HOW TO BECOME A
Better
Man

A Comprehensive Guide to Personal Growth and Leadership

Written by: Isaiah Reid

Contents

Introduction:

What does it really mean to be a better man? Is it about playing by society's rules, chasing status, or pretending to have it all together? Not even close. Becoming a better man isn't about fitting into a box it's about breaking out of one. It's a personal journey of growth, purpose, and self-awareness. No fake masks. No outdated stereotypes. Just real work, real progress, and real results.

This isn't about comparing yourself to anyone else; it's about owning your story. This journey is yours, regardless of your race, ethnicity, background, or where you come from, what you've gone through, or where you're headed. The goal is to learn from your past, show up fully in the present, and create a future you're proud to call your own.

Inside these chapters, you'll find actionable advice, thought-provoking exercises, and real-life examples to inspire your journey on everything from emotional intelligence and leadership to resilience and self-discipline. It's raw, honest, and designed to help you grow.

Growth takes time, effort, and reflection. But with consistency and the right mindset, you'll discover that self improvement is not just a goal; it's a lifelong commitment. Becoming a better man isn't a one-time decision-it's a daily choice. And if you're ready to rise, reflect, and put in the work then turn the page. Your journey of becoming the example starts now.

Let's take the
first step
together.

"Each sunrise invites you to redefine your existence, step beyond your limits, dismantle the familiar, and unleash your inner brilliance."

INSPIRED BY RALPH WALDO EMERSON

Chapter

01.

Reinventing Yourself: Unlocking Your Potential

Reinvention is not about becoming someone entirely new; it's about shedding outdated versions of yourself, embracing change, and aligning with who you truly want to be. Reinventing yourself means breaking free from limiting beliefs, habits, and identities that no longer serve you. It's a process of transformation one that requires courage, self-awareness, and intentional action.

Why Reinvention Matters

Change is a second chance, but growth is a choice. Reinventing yourself allows you to take control of your narrative. It's a powerful way to evolve as a person, adapt to challenges, and move closer to your potential. When you reinvent yourself, you create space for new opportunities, stronger relationships, and a deeper sense of purpose.

Step 1:

Take Inventory of Your Current Self

Before you can reinvent yourself, you must understand where you currently stand.

SELF-REFLECTION QUESTIONS:

❓ Who am I today, and am I satisfied with this version of myself?

❓ What habits, behaviors, or beliefs are holding me back?

❓ What areas of my life need the most change physical, emotional, mental, or spiritual?

➡ **Action:** Write down three aspects of your life you're proud of and three you want to improve. This exercise will provide clarity on where to focus your efforts.

Step 2:

Define the New You

Reinvention starts with a vision. Who do you want to become?

➲ **Visualization Exercise:** Imagine yourself five years from now. What kind of man do you see? How do you speak, act, and interact with others? What does your daily routine look like?

➲ **Action:** Write a "future-self statement," describing the man you aspire to be. For example: "I am a man of integrity, discipline, and kindness. I show up for myself and others, pursue my goals relentlessly, and live with purpose."

Step 3:

Identify and Break Old Patterns

Reinvention requires letting go of habits, relationships, or thought patterns that no longer align with your vision.

➲ **Audit Your Habits:** Make a list of daily habits and ask yourself, Does this habit help or hinder my growth?

➲ **Reframe Negative Beliefs:** Challenge any beliefs that say, I can't change or It's too late for me. Replace them with empowering affirmations like, I am capable of change, and every day is a new opportunity.

Step 4:

Develop New Habits and Skills

Growth comes from action. To reinvent yourself, you must consistently align your actions with your vision.

➲ **Start Small:** Identify one new habit to adopt each week. For example:

➲ Practice gratitude daily.

➲ Wake up 30 minutes earlier to focus on self-care.

➲ Exercise consistently.

➲ **Invest in Yourself:** Take courses, read books, or seek mentorship in areas where you want to grow. Building new skills enhances your confidence and reinforces your transformation.

Step 5:

Surround Yourself with Support

The people around you play a critical role in your reinvention.

➲ **Evaluate Your Circle:** Are the people in your life supporting your growth or holding you back?

➲ **Seek Accountability:** Share your goals with someone you trust. A mentor, coach, or accountability partner can help keep you on track.

➲ **Find Your Tribe:** Surround yourself with like-minded individuals who inspire and challenge you to be better.

Embrace Discomfort and Stay Consistent

Reinvention is not easy. It requires stepping outside your comfort zone and pushing through resistance.

⊙ **Mindset Shift:** See challenges as opportunities to grow rather than obstacles to avoid.

⊙ **Celebrate Small Wins:** Acknowledge your progress, no matter how small. This builds momentum and keeps you motivated.

⊙ **Stay Consistent:** True change happens through consistent effort. Even if you stumble, get back on track and keep moving forward.

Real-Life Example:
A Story of Reinvention

Growing up in the small town of Macon, Georgia, felt like being trapped in a crab bucket. Every time someone tried to climb out, it seemed like others would pull them right back down. As a kid, I was surrounded by poverty and struggle. I remember nights when we didn't know where our next meal would come from, and mornings waking up in places that didn't feel like home. I often wore my friends' clothes to school, doing my best to hide the reality of our situation. Skipping school became the norm, and my friends and I would roam the streets, searching for something anything that gave us a sense of purpose.

Despite the chaos, I held onto dreams of a better life. I used to flip through magazines, captivated by images of success and stories of people who had overcome adversity. Those pages became my escape, fueling my desire to rise above my circumstances. I aspired to be the kind of man people looked up to someone others wanted to be around and learn from.

My friends and I were always getting into trouble, and it was only a matter of time before it all caught up to us. Eventually, it did. In the middle school, my friend and I were caught stealing school clothes from a Walmart. We were on our way to the juvenile detention center when I made a desperate plea to the officers. I told them that if they let us go, we would join the military and turn our lives around. I'm not even sure why I said the military it just came out in the heat of the moment. I could tell the officer didn't believe a word I was saying, but for some reason, he decided to give us a second chance. That day changed everything. And I meant what I said I took that second chance seriously.

I knew that to change my life's trajectory, I had to take full accountability for my actions and circumstances. It wasn't easy to let go of the blame I had placed on my past and family, but I realized that my future was mine to shape. With guidance from my elders and a growing commitment to discipline and structure, I began to see my life take a positive turn.

I dedicated myself to developing new habits and shifting my mindset, prioritizing goal-setting and consistency. To reinforce this transformation, I sought out positive influences and mentorship from people who had overcome struggles of their own. Their wisdom was invaluable. I made it a priority to build self-discipline and routine into my everyday life.

I understood that knowledge and hard work would be the keys to my success. I invested time in learning new skills, taking on jobs, and staying focused on growth. Through constant self-reflection, I also worked to become someone my family could be proud of.

As my life began to improve, I noticed a change in how I carried myself and how others saw me. My mindset matured, my confidence grew, and I became laser-focused on building a better future not just for me, but for the people I cared about. I realized that becoming the example was the best way to inspire others to see what a better version of themselves could look like.

It's safe to say I kept my promise. Seven years later, I enlisted in the U.S. Army, and I'm proud to say that I'm still serving today.

Action Plan: Reinventing Yourself

1. Reflect on where you are today and identify areas for improvement.

2. Write a clear vision of the man you want to become.

3. Identify habits and beliefs to let go of and replace them with new ones.

4. Set one small, achievable goal to start your reinvention journey.

5. Find an accountability partner or mentor to support your growth.

6. Commit to daily, consistent actions that align with your vision.

Closing Thought

Reinvention is not a one-time event it's an ongoing process. Every day, you have the power to make choices that bring you closer to the man you want to be. The journey may not always be easy, but it will be worth it. Remember, the best version of yourself is waiting it's time to meet him.

"Make your life a fortress of truth; when your actions shine with honesty, others can't help but follow."

INSPIRED BY C.S. LEWIS

Chapter

02:

Building a Life of Integrity and Accountability

Integrity and accountability are the cornerstones of being a better man. They form the foundation for trust, respect, and credibility in your relationships, career, and personal life. Living with integrity means being true to your values, making ethical decisions, and following through on your commitments. Accountability means taking responsibility for your actions both successes and mistakes and using them as opportunities for growth.

This chapter explores why these traits matter, how to embody them, and how they can transform your life.

What Is Integrity?

Integrity is the alignment of your words, actions, and values. It's about doing the right thing, even when no one is watching.

WHY INTEGRITY MATTERS:

- **Builds trust:** People are drawn to those they can rely on.

- **Creates self-respect:** Living authentically fosters confidence and self-worth.

- **Sets an example:** A man of integrity inspires others to act with honor.

What Is Accountability?

Accountability is the willingness to accept responsibility for your actions and decisions. It's about owning your mistakes, learning from them, and taking steps to improve.

WHY ACCOUNTABILITY MATTERS:

- **Fosters growth:** Taking ownership allows you to identify areas for self-improvement.

- **Strengthens relationships:** Admitting faults and making amends builds stronger bonds.

- **Encourages discipline:** Accountability keeps you aligned with your goals and values.

Step 1:

Define Your Core Values

Living with integrity starts with knowing what you stand for. Your values guide your decisions and actions.

- ➡ **Reflection Exercise:** Write down your top five values. Examples might include honesty, respect, family, loyalty, or personal growth.

- ➡ **Action:** For each value, write a statement about how you will live it. For example: "I value honesty, so I will always speak the truth, even when it's difficult."

Step 2:

Align Your Actions with Your Words

Integrity requires consistency between what you say and what you do.

- ➡ **Self-Audit:** Reflect on whether your actions match your words. Ask yourself:

- ➡ Am I keeping my promises to others and myself?

- ➡ Do my daily habits align with my values?

- ➡ **Action:** Identify one area where your actions don't align with your values and create a plan to address it. For example, if you value health but neglect exercise, commit to a fitness routine.

Step 3:

Take Responsibility for Your Mistakes

Accountability means owning up to your errors without making excuses.

⊙ Mindset Shift: Understand that mistakes don't define you they are growth opportunities.

ACTION PLAN FOR ACCOUNTABILITY:

1. Admit the mistake.

2. Apologize to anyone affected.

3. Identify what you can learn from the situation.

4. Create a plan to avoid repeating it in the future.

Step 4:

Surround Yourself with Accountability Partners

No man can succeed alone. Building a network of people who hold you accountable can keep you on track.

⊙ Choose Wisely: Surround yourself with individuals who inspire you to be better and who will call you out when you're slipping.

⊙ Regular Check-Ins: Share your goals with a trusted friend, mentor, or group and schedule regular check-ins to discuss your progress.

Make Integrity a Daily Practice

Integrity isn't a one-time choice; it's a habit you cultivate through small, consistent actions.

➔ Daily Habits to Build Integrity:

➔ Speak the truth, even in uncomfortable situations.

➔ Follow through on your commitments.

➔ Treat everyone with respect, regardless of their status.

➔ Reflection Exercise: At the end of each day, ask yourself:

➔ Did I act in alignment with my values today?

➔ Where can I improve tomorrow?

Be Honest About Your Limitations

A key part of accountability is recognizing when you need help or support.

➔ **Self-Awareness Exercise:** List areas of your life where you feel stuck or need improvement.

➔ **Action:** Seek guidance from mentors, counselors, or trusted friends to work through challenges.

Lead by Example

A life of integrity and accountability isn't just for your benefit it inspires those around you.

- **Be a Role Model:** Whether at work, home or in your community, let your actions demonstrate your values.

- **Teach Accountability:** Encourage others to take responsibility for their actions by modeling it yourself.

Real-Life Example: The Power of Integrity and Accountability

There was a time in my life when I felt utterly stuck. I had no sense of direction, no money, and the thought of not having a purpose constantly weighed on me. I wasn't happy with where I was financially, emotionally, or personally. I looked at my circumstances and blamed everything and everyone around me. I blamed my parents for not giving me a better start in life. I blamed my upbringing for the habits I had developed. I even blamed society for making it harder for people like me to succeed. Deep down, though, I knew those excuses were not serving me. I wasn't moving forward because I wasn't taking responsibility for my own life.

I remember sitting alone in my car, parked in an empty lot, with nothing but my thoughts for company. The silence was deafening, and the weight of my choices pressed heavily on my chest. It was in those moments of solitude that I realized the only person holding me back was me. No one else. I was the one who made excuses instead of taking action. I was the one who avoided accountability, waiting for something or someone else to save me. That realization hit me hard, but it also ignited something inside me. It was time to stop blaming my past and start building my future.

One pivotal moment stands out vividly. While working at a Amazon warehouse, I was responsible for managing inventory. One day, I noticed a discrepancy in the stock count a significant number of items were missing. I had made an error in recording the shipments, which led to a huge loss. Fear gripped me. I knew admitting my mistake could cost me my job. But I also knew that hiding it would compromise my integrity. Summoning courage, I approached my supervisor, explained the situation, and took full responsibility. To my surprise, instead of reprimanding me, he appreciated my honesty and worked with me to rectify the issue. That experience reinforced the importance of owning up to my actions and the respect that comes with it.

That moment in the warehouse, where I chose to admit my mistake, was more than just a professional decision it was a defining point in my personal development. By confronting the error head-on, I demonstrated to myself that I was capable of upholding my values, even when it was uncomfortable. This act of integrity reinforced my self-respect and set a new standard for how I would handle challenges moving forward.

Embracing accountability meant acknowledging my role in both successes and failures. It required me to move beyond excuses and take ownership of my actions. This shift in mindset was pivotal; it allowed me to learn from my experiences and make conscious efforts to improve. As I consistently applied these principles, I noticed a change in how I approached decisions, interacted with others, and viewed myself.

Over time, these practices became integral to my identity. They influenced my relationships, my work ethic, and my aspirations. I became someone who others could rely on, someone who led by example. This transformation wasn't about perfection but about progress continually striving to align my actions with my values. In essence, choosing integrity and accountability didn't just rectify a single mistake; it initiated a journey of personal growth that reshaped my life. It taught me that being a better man isn't about never faltering but about how we respond when we do. It's about facing ourselves honestly, learning from our missteps, and committing to do better not just for ourselves, but for those we influence.

Action Plan: Building Integrity and Accountability

1. Define your top five values and write a commitment statement for each.

2. Identify areas where your actions don't align with your words, and create a plan to address them.

3. Start a daily reflection practice to evaluate whether you lived with integrity that day.

4. Find an accountability partner to share your goals and track your progress.

5. When you make a mistake, follow the four-step process: admit it, apologize, learn from it, and improve.

6. Take one small action each day that reflects your commitment to integrity and accountability.

Closing Thought

Living with integrity and accountability is not about being perfect it's about being honest, consistent, and willing to grow. These qualities will earn you the respect of others, deepen your relationships, and help you lead a life you can be proud of. Each day offers a new chance to show up as the man you want to be. Embrace it.

"Time bows to the disciplined soul shape every moment with purpose, and you'll become the architect of your destiny."

INSPIRED BY TONY ROBBINS

Chapter

03:

Mastering Self-Discipline and Time Management

Success in any area of life requires self-discipline and effective time management. These two skills are interconnected: discipline helps you stay consistent in your actions, while time management ensures you make the most of your efforts. Together, they empower you to achieve your goals, improve productivity, and create balance in your life.

In this chapter, you'll learn strategies to strengthen your self-discipline, manage your time effectively, and develop habits that lead to long-term success.

What Is Self-Discipline?

Self-discipline is the ability to control your impulses, stay focused on your priorities, and follow through on commitments, even when motivation wanes.

WHY IT MATTERS:

➔ **Builds consistency:** Discipline keeps you moving forward, even on hard days.

➔ **Promotes growth:** Helps you resist distractions and focus on meaningful tasks.

➔ **Boosts confidence:** Each disciplined action strengthens your belief in your ability to succeed.

What Is Time Management?

Time management is the process of planning and controlling how you allocate your time to specific activities.

WHY IT MATTERS:

➔ **Increases productivity:** Helps you focus on high-priority tasks.

➔ **Reduces stress:** Keeps you organized and prevents last-minute scrambling.

➔ **Creates balance:** Ensures you dedicate time to work, relationships, and self-care.

Step 1:

Clarify Your Goals and Priorities

Effective self-discipline and time management begin with a clear sense of purpose.

➤ Set SMART Goals: Goals should be Specific, Measurable, Achievable, Relevant, and Time-bound.

➤ Example: Instead of "Get in shape," say, "Lose 10 pounds in 3 months by exercising 4 times a week and eating healthier."

➤ Identify Priorities: List the top 3–5 areas of your life that matter most (e.g., career, family, health, personal growth).

Step 2:

Create a Daily Routine

Discipline thrives on structure. A well-designed routine helps you stay consistent and focused.

➤ Morning Routine: Start your day with intentional habits, such as meditation, exercise, or reviewing your goals.

➤ Evening Routine: Reflect on your progress, plan for the next day, and wind down with activities that promote relaxation.

➤ Daily Schedule: Break your day into time blocks for specific tasks, such as work, exercise, and leisure.

Step 3:

Develop Strong Habits

Habits are the building blocks of self-discipline. The more automatic your positive habits become, the less energy you'll spend on willpower.

➤ **Start Small:** Focus on one habit at a time to avoid overwhelm.

➤ **Example:** Commit to a 10-minute workout each day before aiming for a full hour.

➤ **Track Your Progress:** Use a habit tracker or journal to monitor your consistency.

➤ **Reward Yourself:** Celebrate small wins to reinforce your new habits.

Step 4:

Manage Your Time Effectively

Time management is about working smarter, not harder. Use these strategies to make the most of your time:

➤ **The Eisenhower Matrix:** Categorize tasks into four quadrants:

1. Urgent and Important: Do these immediately.

2. Important but Not Urgent: Schedule these for later.

3. Urgent but Not Important: Delegate or minimize these.

4. Neither Urgent nor Important: Eliminate these tasks.

➤ **The 80/20 Rule (Pareto Principle):** Focus on the 20% of tasks that generate 80% of your results.

➤ **Batch Similar Tasks:** Group similar activities, like responding to emails or running errands, to save time.

Overcome Procrastination

Procrastination is a common obstacle to both self-discipline and time management.

➔ **Identify Triggers:** Reflect on why you procrastinate fear of failure, lack of motivation, or feeling overwhelmed.

➔ **Break Tasks Into Smaller Steps:** Large tasks can feel daunting. Divide them into manageable chunks.

➔ **Example:** Instead of "Write a report," break it into:

1. Research the topic.
2. Create an outline.
3. Write the introduction.

➔ **Use the 5-Minute Rule:** Commit to working on a task for just five minutes. Often, you'll build momentum to keep going.

Eliminate Distractions

Distractions derail focus and productivity.

➔ **Identify Time-Wasters:** Track how you spend your time to spot activities that don't align with your goals (e.g., excessive social media use).

➔ Create a Focused Environment:

➔ Turn off notifications on your devices.

➔ Use apps like Freedom or Focus@Will to block distractions.

➔ Work in a quiet, organized space.

➔ **Practice Deep Work:** Dedicate uninterrupted time to tasks that require concentration.

Stay Consistent and Adaptable

Consistency is the key to mastering self-discipline and time management, but flexibility is also important.

‣ **Review and Adjust:** Regularly evaluate your routines and goals to ensure they align with your priorities.

‣ **Learn From Setbacks:** If you slip up, don't dwell on it. Reflect on what went wrong and adjust your approach.

Understand Delayed Gratification

Delayed gratification is the ability to resist immediate rewards in favor of long-term success. Mastering this skill is essential for achieving meaningful goals and maintaining self-discipline.

The Importance of Delayed Gratification

‣ Helps build stronger self-control and willpower.

‣ Encourages long-term thinking, leading to better decision-making.

‣ Reduces impulsive behaviors that can lead to setbacks in finances, health, and relationships.

The Benefits of Delayed Gratification

1. **Greater Success & Achievement**

> Those who practice patience and discipline often outperform others in career, business, and personal growth.

2. **Stronger Financial Stability**

> Avoiding instant spending leads to better savings, investments, and overall financial security.

3. **Improved Physical & Mental Health**

> Choosing long-term health over short-term pleasure leads to better fitness, nutrition, and mental well-being.

4. **Better Relationships**

> Practicing patience fosters deeper, more meaningful connections instead of seeking quick validation.

5. **Increased Confidence**

> Learning to wait and work toward goals strengthens mental toughness and self-belief.

Real-Life Example: The Power of Discipline and Time Management

Society often underestimates the profound impact a man can have on a child's life or even on another man's. In my case, that influence came at a time when I was spiraling. Disregarding my mother's authority and command. Raising seven kids alone as a single mother was already a challenge, but my added headache at times made it even tougher. I was simply taking advantage of the fact that it was just her and no male figure present in our household. My days were consumed by distractions, my nights by aimless wandering, and my future seemed like a distant mirage. I was adrift, lacking purpose and direction.

Then Johnny Gordon entered our lives. My mother met him at a church where she volunteered cleaning the church as a form of her tithing. He and his wife, Leila, became like a second set of parents to me and my younger brother Javiee. Johnny was a man of unwavering discipline and structure. He saw through my excuses and confronted me with a level of honesty I hadn't encountered before. His presence was both challenging and comforting, a beacon guiding me toward a better path. Johnny didn't just preach discipline; he lived it. His days began before dawn, each moment accounted for, each task executed with precision. He maintained a meticulous schedule: early morning grooming, structured work hours, and designated worship time. Even though he was retired you would think he had a full time job. His life was a testament to the power of routine and commitment.

Observing Johnny, I learned the importance of honoring one's commitments, no matter how small. He taught me to wake up early, to plan my day, and to stick to my goals. His consistent actions built a foundation of trust and respect, not just from others, but within himself. Johnny's integrity was evident in every aspect of his life, making him a role model worth emulating. Implementing his teachings brought tangible changes to my life. By adopting a structured routine, I began to see improvements in my productivity and focus. Waking up early allowed me to start the day with intention, setting a positive tone for the hours ahead. Prioritizing tasks helped me manage my time effectively, reducing stress and increasing my sense of accomplishment.

Research supports these experiences. Effective time management and self-discipline are linked to increased productivity, better goal attainment, and reduced stress. By aligning my actions with my goals, I was able to make steady progress toward becoming the man I aspired to be. Johnny's influence was transformative. Through his example, I learned that discipline and time management are not just tools for success, but expressions of self-respect and integrity. His mentorship illuminated a path forward, turning my life upside down but in a good way. Today, I carry his lessons with me, striving to live with the same dedication and honor that he exemplified.

Action Plan: Mastering Self-Discipline and Time Management

1. Define your SMART goals and top priorities.

2. Design a daily routine with time blocks for important tasks.

3. Focus on building one new habit at a time and track your progress.

4. Use tools like the Eisenhower Matrix or the 80/20 Rule to prioritize tasks.

5. Break big tasks into smaller steps to overcome procrastination.

6. Eliminate distractions and create an environment that supports focus.

7. Reflect on your progress weekly and adjust as needed.

Closing Thought

Self-discipline and time management are not innate talents they're skills you can develop with practice and patience. By mastering these skills, you'll not only achieve your goals but also build a life of purpose, balance, and fulfillment. Remember, every disciplined choice you make today shapes the man you'll become tomorrow. Start now.

"Treat your body as a cherished sanctuary; every act of care is a bold declaration of self-respect."

INSPIRED BY DEEPAK CHOPRA

Chapter

04:

The Foundations of Hygiene and Personal Care

Hygiene and personal care are fundamental aspects of being a better man. How you present yourself reflects your respect for yourself and others. Good hygiene boosts your confidence, improves your health, and leaves a positive impression on the people you interact with. It's not about vanity; it's about self-respect, discipline, and maintaining high standards.

In this chapter, you'll learn how to build and maintain an effective hygiene and grooming routine, from head to toe, while understanding the deeper importance of personal care.

Why Hygiene and Personal Care Matter

➔ **Health Benefits:** Proper hygiene prevents illnesses, infections, and skin conditions.

➔ **Confidence Boost:** When you look and feel your best, it enhances your self-esteem.

➔ **Social and Professional Impact:** A well-groomed appearance leaves a strong, positive impression in personal and professional settings.

Step 1:

Build a Daily Hygiene Routine

Consistency is the key to maintaining proper hygiene. Below is a step-by-step guide to creating a solid routine.

Morning Routine

1. **Shower Daily:**

> Use warm water and a gentle body wash or soap that suits your skin type.

> Pay special attention to areas prone to sweating, such as underarms and groin.

> Avoid over-scrubbing, as it can dry out your skin.

2. Brush and Floss Your Teeth:

> Make sure to brush twice a day for at least two minutes with a toothpaste that offers cavity prevention, whitening, and fresh breath.

> Floss twice daily or after every meal to remove plaque and food particles between your teeth.

> Consider using mouthwash for added freshness.

3. Deodorant or Antiperspirant:

> Choose a product that works for your skin type and provides lasting protection against odor.

4. Skincare Basics:

> Cleanse your face with a facial cleanser suited to your skin type (oily, dry, or combination).

> Apply moisturizer with SPF to protect your skin from UV damage.

Evening Routine

1. Wash Your Face:

> Remove dirt, oil, and pollutants accumulated throughout the day with a gentle cleanser.

2. Floss and Brush Again:

> Evening dental care is essential for preventing cavities and gum disease.

3. Moisturize:

> Apply a hydrating moisturizer or serum to nourish your skin overnight.

Step 2:

Hair Care

Healthy hair contributes significantly to your overall appearance.

➲ **Shampoo and Condition:**

> ❯ Wash your hair 2–3 times per week with a shampoo that suits your hair type.

> ❯ Use conditioner to keep your hair soft and manageable.

➲ **Scalp Care:**

> ❯ If you have dandruff, use a medicated shampoo.

> ❯ Massage your scalp during washing to improve circulation and promote hair growth.

➲ **Styling Products:**

> ❯ Use products like pomade, gel, or wax sparingly to avoid buildup.

> ❯ Choose styles that suit your face shape and lifestyle.

Step 3:

Nail Care

Neglected nails can leave a poor impression and harbor bacteria.

➲ **Trim Regularly:**

> ❯ Keep fingernails and toenails short and clean.

> ❯ Trim nails straight across to avoid ingrown nails.

➲ **Clean Underneath:**

> ❯ Use a nail brush to remove dirt from under your nails.

➲ **Moisturize Cuticles:**

> ❯ Prevent dryness and cracking by applying cuticle oil or lotion.

Step 4:

Body Hair Grooming

Grooming body hair is a personal preference, but maintaining cleanliness is non-negotiable.

➔ **Beards and Facial Hair:**
> Trim or shave regularly, depending on your style.
> Use beard oil or balm to keep your facial hair soft and hydrated.

➔ **Underarms and Groin:**
> Keep these areas clean and trimmed to reduce odor and sweating.
> Avoid harsh products that can irritate sensitive skin.

➔ **Chest, Back, and Legs:**
> Groom these areas as desired, using clippers or razors designed for body hair.

Step 5:

Foot Care

Your feet endure a lot every day and require proper attention.

➔ **Wash and Dry Thoroughly:**
> Clean your feet daily, especially between the toes, to prevent fungal infections.
> Dry them well after washing.

➔ **Wear Fresh Socks:**
> Change socks daily to reduce odor and moisture buildup.
> Use moisture-wicking socks if you sweat excessively.

➔ **Exfoliate and Moisturize:**
> Remove dead skin with a pumice stone or foot scrub.
> Apply foot cream to prevent cracked heels.

Step 6:

Invest in Personal Care Products

Choosing the right products can make a significant difference in your hygiene routine.

⊙ Essentials:

> Body wash or soap

> Shampoo and conditioner

> Face cleanser and moisturizer

> Deodorant or antiperspirant

> Razor and shaving cream or gel

> Nail clippers and file

> Toothbrush, toothpaste, and floss

⊙ Optional Additions:

> **Cologne:** My personal favorites are Mohave Ghost by Byredo, Moon Glory by Harmonist, and Vert Intense by Prismè

> Beard oil or balm

> Sunscreen for outdoor activities

Hygiene Habits Beyond the Basics

❯ **Laundry:**

> ❯ Wear clean clothes every day, especially undergarments and socks.

> ❯ Wash your bedding regularly, particularly pillowcases, to prevent acne and allergies.

❯ **Hand Hygiene:**

> ❯ Wash your hands frequently, especially before meals and after using the restroom.

> ❯ Use hand sanitizer when soap and water aren't available.

❯ **Regular Grooming Appointments:**

> ❯ Schedule haircuts every 1-3 weeks to maintain a polished look. Self-grooming is always an option to stay well-kept more frequently.

> ❯ Visit a dentist twice a year for checkups and cleanings.

Explore Cosmetic Improvements:

❯ Non-Invasive Enhancements

> ❯ Botox ("Brotox"): Reduces the appearance of fine lines and wrinkles, particularly on the forehead and around the eyes, resulting in a more youthful look. I know there is a preserved notion about Botox for men but it's just for aging that's it

> ❯ Laser Skin Resurfacing: Improves skin texture and tone by addressing issues like acne scars, sun damage, and uneven pigmentation.

> ❯ Microneedling: Stimulates collagen production, reducing the appearance of scars and fine lines for smoother skin.

> ❯ Chemical Peels: Exfoliate the skin to reveal a fresher, more radiant complexion.

➔ Surgical Procedures

> Facelift: Tightens sagging facial tissues, providing a more youthful and refreshed appearance.

> Hair Transplantation: Addresses hair loss by relocating hair follicles to thinning or balding areas, restoring a fuller hairline.

➔ Dental Enhancements

> Teeth Whitening: Brightens your smile by removing stains and discoloration, boosting confidence.

> Dental Veneers: Thin porcelain shells placed over the front of teeth to correct imperfections like chips, gaps, or discoloration, providing a flawless appearance.

> Orthodontic Treatments: Aligns and straightens teeth using braces or clear aligners, improving both function and aesthetics.

➔ Grooming and Aesthetic Practices

> Eyebrow Grooming: Well-shaped eyebrows frame the face and can enhance overall appearance.

> Beard Styling: A well-maintained beard can define facial features and convey a polished look.

> Skincare Regimen: Regular cleansing, moisturizing, and sun protection maintain healthy and youthful skin.

Facials: Professional facials offer deep cleansing, exfoliation, and hydration tailored to men's skin, which tends to be thicker and oilier. Benefits include unclogging pores, reducing acne, and promoting smoother skin. Facials can also alleviate shaving irritation and ingrown hairs, enhancing overall skin health and appearance.

Real-Life Example: The Confidence of Good Hygiene

Your perception is everything. In social settings, I struggled to connect with others. Conversations were challenging, friendships were scarce, and romantic interests seemed to overlook me. Deep down, I knew part of this stemmed from neglecting my personal hygiene and grooming. I didn't prioritize self-care, and it showed not just to others, but to myself. This realization hit me hard. I yearned for change, for a sense of confidence and belonging. That's when I turned to the examples set by two influential men in my life: Johnny Gordon, my second dad, and my biological father, Vernon Reid. Both carried themselves with dignity, always well-groomed and polished. Their presence commanded respect, not because of designer clothes, but because they took pride in their appearance. Sadly, they are no longer with us. May their souls rest in peace.

Growing up, I watched my father glide through life with a sense of purpose and a scent of fresh cologne that lingered long after he left the room. He wasn't just well-dressed; he was dapper, every day. Shoes shined. Beard trimmed. Nails clean. A bald head that was actually a mirror you could see yourself in. Even in his casual clothes, he carried himself with an elegance that demanded respect. I didn't realize it then, but he was modeling something far greater than style he was teaching me discipline, self-respect, and the unspoken language of appearance. When I speak to you about hygiene and grooming, it's not theory. It's a lived practice, a generational torch passed from father to son. I am simply continuing the legacy of excellence he embedded in me. I remember being a kid, sitting on the edge of the tub, watching him lather his face with shaving cream. It was more than a routine it was a ritual. One that told me: You are worth the time. You are worth the effort. That memory stayed with me. Every time I take care of myself, I feel him there, reminding me that how we present ourselves tells the world how we feel inside.

Studies show that people who practice consistent hygiene and grooming routines report higher levels of self-confidence, lower stress, and greater success in social and professional settings. It's not vanity it's strategy. Cleanliness communicates trustworthiness. A neat appearance signals attention to detail. The logic is simple: when you look good, you feel good, and when you feel good, you perform better. Inspired by Johnny and Vernon, I decided to mirror their habits. I overhauled my hygiene routine, paid attention to how I dressed, and ensured I always looked and felt presentable. Growing up in a lower-class environment, I never grasped the idea of wearing fancy designer clothes. But I made a commitment to myself: I didn't need designer labels. As long as my clothes were clean, ironed, and presentable, I could wear them with confidence.

The change was immediate. People started noticing me more, treating me with respect, and I felt a surge of confidence I had never experienced before. By prioritizing self-care, I transformed how I viewed myself and how others viewed me. It was a simple change, but it completely reshaped my social interactions and how I showed up in the world. It's not what you wear; it's how you wear it that makes a difference. By adopting a consistent grooming routine, I not only improved my health but also enhanced my self-esteem. This transformation underscored the profound impact that self-care can have on one's life. I discovered a newfound confidence and a deeper respect for myself. This journey taught me that self-care is not a luxury but a fundamental aspect of personal growth and social connection.

Action Plan: Building Your Hygiene Routine

1. Assess your current hygiene habits and identify areas for improvement.

2. Create a daily routine for morning and evening hygiene.

3. Invest in quality personal care products that suit your needs.

4. Commit to regular grooming and maintenance, from haircuts to nail care.

5. Schedule reminders for weekly and monthly hygiene tasks, like exfoliating or laundry.

Closing Thought

Hygiene and personal care are not just about looking good they're about feeling good, staying healthy, and showing respect for yourself and others. By building strong hygiene habits, you'll enhance your confidence, improve your well-being, and create a positive impression wherever you go. A better man begins with how you care for yourself.

"You can have 1,000 problems in life until you have a health problem, and then you only have one problem."

INSPIRED BY ISAIAH REID

Chapter

05:

Physical Health and Longevity: The Key to a Stronger, Healthier Future

Your physical health is the foundation of your overall well-being. A strong, healthy body enables you to pursue your goals, handle challenges, and enjoy life to the fullest. Focusing on longevity isn't just about living longer it's about living better, with vitality and strength that lasts into old age.

This chapter delves into the key elements of maintaining physical health and promoting longevity, including exercise, nutrition, sleep, and preventative care. You'll gain actionable strategies to build a healthier lifestyle and set yourself up for long-term success.

The Importance of Physical Health

➔ **Energy and Productivity:** A healthy body improves your energy levels, focus, and efficiency in daily tasks.

➔ **Resilience:** Regular exercise and proper nutrition enhance your ability to cope with stress and recover from illness or injury.

➔ **Quality of Life:** Maintaining physical health allows you to stay active and independent as you age.

Step 1:

Develop a Balanced Exercise Routine

Exercise is essential for building strength, improving endurance, and promoting cardiovascular health. A balanced routine includes aerobic activity, strength training, flexibility, and rest.

1. **Aerobic (Cardio) Exercise**
> **Benefits:** Improves heart health, boosts stamina, and burns calories.
> **Examples:** Running, cycling, swimming, or brisk walking.
> **Recommendation:** Aim for at least 150 minutes of moderate-intensity cardio or 75 minutes of vigorous cardio per week.

2. **Strength Training**

> **Benefits:** Builds muscle, strengthens bones, and increases metabolism.

> **Examples:** Weightlifting, resistance bands, or bodyweight exercises like push-ups and squats.

> **Recommendation:** Train all major muscle groups 2–3 times per week, allowing at least one rest day between sessions.

3. **Flexibility and Mobility**

> **Benefits:** Prevents injuries, reduces stiffness, and improves posture.

> **Examples:** Stretching, yoga, or Pilates.

> **Recommendation:** Incorporate 10–15 minutes of stretching after workouts or on rest days.

4. **Rest and Recovery**

> **Importance:** Overtraining can lead to fatigue and injuries. Rest days allow your body to repair and grow stronger.

> **Action:** Schedule 1–2 rest days per week and prioritize active recovery activities like light walks or stretching.

Step 2:

Prioritize Nutrition

What you eat plays a critical role in your physical health and longevity. Fuel your body with the nutrients it needs to perform and recover.

1. **Focus on Whole Foods**

> Choose nutrient-dense foods like vegetables, fruits, lean proteins, whole grains, and healthy fats.

> Minimize processed foods, added sugars, and trans fats.

2. **Balanced Macronutrients**

> **Proteins:** Build and repair muscles. Include sources like chicken, fish, eggs, legumes, and tofu.

- ❯ **Carbohydrates:** Provide energy. Opt for complex carbs like brown rice, quinoa, and oats.
- ❯ **Fats:** Support brain function and hormone production. Include healthy fats like avocados, nuts, seeds, and olive oil.

3. Portion Control

- ❯ Avoid overeating by being mindful of portion sizes. Use smaller plates and listen to your body's hunger and fullness cues.

4. Hydration

- ❯ Drink plenty of water throughout the day to support digestion, circulation, and overall health.
- ❯ **Recommendation:** Aim for at least 8–10 cups of water daily, more if you're active.

5. Supplements (If Needed)

- ❯ Consider supplements like vitamin D, omega-3s, or multivitamins if your diet lacks essential nutrients. Consult a healthcare professional first.

6. Incorporate Juicing for an Extra Nutritional Boost

- ❯ **Enhanced Nutrient Absorption:** Juicing extracts a concentrated blend of vitamins, minerals, and antioxidants from fruits and vegetables, making them easier for your body to absorb quickly.
- ❯ **Increased Fruit and Vegetable Intake:** If you find it challenging to consume the recommended daily servings of produce, juicing offers a convenient way to boost your intake and ensure you get a wide range of nutrients.
- ❯ **Detoxification Support:** Fresh juices can help support your body's natural detox processes by providing hydration and supplying antioxidants that combat free radicals.
- ❯ **Improved Digestion:** Since juicing breaks down the fiber, the nutrients become more bioavailable. This can lead to improved digestion and relief for those with sensitive stomachs.
- ❯ **Energy Boost:** A nutrient-rich juice can quickly elevate your energy levels and overall vitality, supporting active lifestyles and faster recovery after workouts.

Overall, incorporating fresh juices into your diet should help promote clearer skin, better immune function, and assist with weight management when used as a complement to whole foods. Remember, while juicing offers many benefits, it's best used to supplement a balanced diet that still includes whole fruits and vegetables for their fiber content.

Step 3:

Optimize Sleep

Sleep is the body's time to recover, repair, and recharge. Poor sleep negatively impacts your energy, focus, and overall health.

1. **Establish a Sleep Schedule**
> Go to bed and wake up at the same time every day, even on weekends.

2. **Create a Sleep-Friendly Environment**
> Keep your bedroom cool, dark, and quiet.
> Avoid screens (phones, tablets, TVs) at least 1 hour before bedtime to minimize blue light exposure.

3. **Aim for Quality Sleep**
> **Recommendation:** Adults should aim for 7–9 hours of sleep per night.
> Practice relaxation techniques like deep breathing or meditation if you have trouble falling asleep.

Step 4:

Preventative Healthcare

Staying proactive about your health can prevent serious conditions and detect potential issues early.

1. **Regular Checkups**

> Schedule annual physical exams to monitor blood pressure, cholesterol, and overall health.

> Address any health concerns with your doctor promptly.

2. **Immunizations**

> Stay up to date on vaccinations, including flu shots and other recommended immunizations.

3. **Screenings**

> Depending on your age, undergo regular screenings for conditions like diabetes, cancer, or heart disease.

Step 5:

Manage Stress

Chronic stress can take a toll on your physical health, contributing to conditions like high blood pressure, weight gain, and weakened immunity.

1. **Stress-Reduction Techniques**

> Practice mindfulness or meditation.
> Engage in hobbies or activities that bring you joy.
> Exercise regularly to release endorphins and reduce tension.

2. **Build a Support System**

> Stay connected with friends and family who uplift you.

> Don't hesitate to seek professional help if needed, such as therapy or counseling.

Step 6:

Avoid Harmful Habits

Longevity depends on avoiding behaviors that harm your body.

⊙ **Quit Smoking:** Smoking significantly increases the risk of chronic diseases. Seek support to quit.

⊙ **Limit Alcohol:** Consume alcohol in moderation no more than 1–2 drinks per day.

⊙ **Avoid Substance Abuse:** Stay away from drugs or misuse of prescription medications.

Step 7:

Stay Consistent and Adapt Over Time

Your physical health needs may change as you age. Be flexible and adapt your routine to fit your evolving lifestyle and goals.

⊙ **Track Your Progress:** Keep a journal of your workouts, meals, and sleep to identify patterns and areas for improvement.

⊙ **Listen to Your Body:** Pay attention to signs of fatigue or discomfort, and adjust your routine accordingly.

Recognize the Healing Power of Food

Our bodies are designed to heal and thrive, and the food we consume is a powerful catalyst in that process. Choosing the right foods isn't just about filling up, it's about providing your body with the nutrients it needs to repair, renew, and protect itself.

➲ **Fuel for Healing:** Every bite you take should supply your body with essential vitamins, minerals, and antioxidants. These nutrients help combat inflammation, reduce oxidative stress, and support the natural repair mechanisms within your cells. A diet rich in whole foods, fruits, vegetables, lean proteins, and whole grains can fortify your immune system and accelerate the healing process.

➲ **Building Blocks for Longevity:** The right diet acts as the foundation for long-term health. When you choose nutrient-dense foods, you're not only fueling your day-to-day energy levels, but you're also laying the groundwork for a healthier future. Consistently eating a balanced diet helps maintain healthy weight, supports cardiovascular health, and reduces the risk of chronic diseases.

➲ **A Natural Prescription:** Your body has an incredible capacity to heal itself, and food is one of the most natural, accessible tools you have to enhance that process. Incorporating anti-inflammatory foods, such as berries, leafy greens, and omega-3 rich fish, can significantly boost your body's innate healing abilities. Conversely, minimizing processed foods and refined sugars can prevent unnecessary stress on your system, allowing your body's repair mechanisms to work more effectively.

➲ **Lifestyle Integration:** Recognizing the healing power of food means understanding that what you eat directly influences your quality of life. By making conscious, informed choices about your diet, you invest in your physical health and overall well-being. A mindful approach to nutrition doesn't just prevent disease it can help you achieve a level of vitality and resilience that empowers you to live your best life.

In embracing this step, you not only support your body's natural healing processes but also set the stage for a lifestyle of vitality and longevity. Your diet is a daily opportunity to nurture yourself, proving that the path to health is paved with every nutritious choice you make.

Real-Life Example: The Journey to Health and Longevity

Everyone wants to be healthy and live and long life but not everyone is willing to do what it takes to preserve life. After leaving the structured environment of military training, my daily routine lacked exercise. My stomach protruded more than I cared to admit, my body ached during simple daily tasks, and I couldn't perform at the level I knew I was capable of. It's easy to stay in shape when you are being woke up everyday being forced to workout. I had to find motivation within and I realized I couldn't keep ignoring my physical health if I wanted to succeed in other areas of my life.

The challenge was overwhelming: finding time to exercise, changing my diet, and staying motivated. But I knew it was time to take control. I began with small commitments regular morning workouts and gradual improvements to my diet. Consistency became my mantra, even on days when motivation waned. I incorporated more whole foods into my meals and cut back on processed junk. Juicing fruits and vegetables became a staple, tapping into my body's natural healing processes and ensuring I stayed nourished.

The changes weren't easy at first, but the results started to show. I had more energy, my mental clarity improved, and I began feeling stronger and more confident in my body. These positive changes didn't just affect my physical health they boosted my overall mood, productivity, and even my relationships. Blood was literally surfing through my body if you know what I mean lol. Adopting healthier habits transformed my life. It wasn't about perfection; it was about progress and committing to a healthier, more vibrant future. In a society that rarely promotes healthy eating and exercise, making these choices requires deliberate effort. But the rewards a longer, healthier life are well worth it.

Action Plan:
Building a Healthier Life

1. Commit to at least 30 minutes of physical activity each day.

2. Replace processed foods with whole, nutrient-dense options.

3. Create a consistent sleep schedule and aim for 7–9 hours of rest per night.

4. Schedule annual checkups and preventative screenings.

5. Identify one harmful habit to eliminate and take steps to address it.

Closing Thought

Physical health is the foundation of a fulfilling life. By prioritizing fitness, nutrition, sleep, and preventative care, you're not only improving your current well-being but also investing in your future. Every step you take today brings you closer to a stronger, healthier, and more vibrant version of yourself. Choose to live with intention, and watch your body reward you with strength and longevity.

"Arm yourself with courage and skill; stand guard for your values and loved ones, and no threat will go unanswered."

INSPIRED BY BRUCE LEE

Chapter

06:

Self-Defense and Safety: Protecting Yourself and Those Around You

I n today's world, prioritizing personal safety is an essential part of being a better man. The ability to protect yourself and those around you is not just about physical strength it's about awareness, preparation, and smart decision-making. This chapter will teach you how to stay safe in various situations, develop effective self-defense skills, and cultivate a mindset of vigilance without living in fear.

The Importance of Self-Defense and Safety

➔ **Protection:** Knowing how to defend yourself can save your life and those of others.

➔ **Confidence:** Being prepared reduces fear and builds self-assurance in unfamiliar or risky situations.

➔ **Empowerment:** Learning self-defense fosters independence and the ability to handle emergencies.

Step 1:

Awareness and Prevention

The best way to stay safe is to avoid dangerous situations altogether. Awareness and prevention are your first lines of defense.

1. **Situational Awareness**
   > Always stay alert and aware of your surroundings.
   > Avoid distractions like texting or wearing headphones in unfamiliar or crowded areas.
   > Learn to identify potential threats, such as suspicious behavior or unsafe environments.

2. **Trust Your Instincts**
   > If something doesn't feel right, trust your gut and remove yourself from the situation.
   > Your instincts are often a subconscious response to subtle cues in your environment.

3. Avoid Risky Situations

> Stay in well-lit, populated areas, especially at night.

> Avoid shortcuts through alleys, deserted streets, or unfamiliar neighborhoods.

> Limit alcohol consumption in public places to maintain control and awareness.

4. Establish Boundaries

> Be clear about your personal space and what behavior you will or won't tolerate.

> Use verbal assertiveness to defuse situations before they escalate.

Step 2:

Basic Self-Defense Techniques

While avoidance is ideal, knowing how to defend yourself physically is crucial in case of an attack. Below are basic self-defense principles and moves.

1. Key Principles of Self-Defense

> **Stay Calm:** Panic can cloud your judgment; focus on breathing and staying composed.

> **Aim for Escape:** The goal of self-defense is to create an opportunity to escape, not to fight.

> **Use the Element of Surprise:** Strike quickly and decisively to catch an attacker off guard.

2. Basic Moves

> **Palm Strike:** Strike the attacker's nose or chin with the heel of your palm.

> **Knee Strike:** Aim for the groin area with your knee to incapacitate the attacker.

> **Elbow Strike:** Use your elbow to target the jaw, ribs, or neck when in close range.

> **Foot Stomp:** Step forcefully on the attacker's foot to cause pain and create an opening for escape.

> **Escape Grabs:**

> If your wrist is grabbed, twist toward the attacker's thumb to break free.

> Use leverage and momentum to free yourself from bear hugs or chokeholds.

3. **Practice Makes Perfect**

> Attend self-defense classes to learn and practice these techniques under professional guidance.

> Consider martial arts training in disciplines like Karate, Brazilian Jiu-Jitsu, or even Boxing, which emphasize real-world scenarios.

Step 3:

Safety Tools and Resources

Carrying safety tools can enhance your ability to protect yourself in emergencies.

1. **Non-Lethal Tools**

> **Pepper Spray:** Compact and easy to use, pepper spray can temporarily disable an attacker.

> **Personal Alarm:** A loud alarm can draw attention and deter potential threats.

> **Tactical Flashlight:** A flashlight can illuminate dark areas and be used to temporarily blind an attacker.

2. **Everyday Objects as Weapons**

> Learn to use items like keys, pens, or a sturdy umbrella as improvised self-defense tools.

3. **Legal Considerations**

> Research local laws regarding self-defense tools, including restrictions on pepper spray, tasers, or other weapons.

Protecting Your Home

Your home should be a safe space. Taking measures to secure it can reduce the risk of break-ins or other threats.

1. **Strengthen Entry Points**

> Install deadbolt locks on doors and ensure windows are secure.

> Use a peephole or security camera to verify visitors before opening the door.

2. **Install a Security System**

> Invest in a home alarm system with motion detectors and cameras.

> Place visible signs or stickers indicating your home is protected.

3. **Keep Your Property Well-Lit**

> Install motion-activated lights around your home's exterior.

> Trim bushes or trees that could provide cover for intruders.

4. **Consider Firearm Ownership for Home Defense**

> If you choose to own a firearm, research your state's laws regarding ownership, storage, and self-defense.

> Take firearm safety courses to ensure responsible handling and usage.

> Store firearms securely to prevent unauthorized access, especially if children are present.

Step 5:

Online Safety

In the digital age, personal safety extends to your online presence. Protect yourself from identity theft, scams, and cyberattacks.

1. Secure Your Accounts

> Use strong, unique passwords for each account and enable two-factor authentication.

> Avoid sharing sensitive information on social media or unsecured websites.

2. Be Cautious Online

> Beware of phishing emails or messages asking for personal information.

> Avoid clicking on suspicious links or downloading unknown files.

3. Monitor Your Financial Accounts

> Regularly check bank statements and credit reports for unauthorized activity.

Step 6:

Emergency Preparedness

Prepare for emergencies to ensure you can respond effectively if the unexpected occurs.

1. Have an Emergency Plan

> Know escape routes from your home or workplace.

> Share your plan with family or roommates and practice regularly.

2. **Carry an Emergency Kit**
> Include essentials like a first aid kit, flashlight, water, and a whistle.

3. **Learn Basic First Aid**
> Take a first aid and CPR course to respond to medical emergencies.

Step 7:

Have a Safety Mindset

Safety is as much about mindset as it is about skills and tools.

1. **Confidence and Posture**
> Walk with purpose and confidence; attackers are less likely to target someone who looks alert and assertive.

2. **De-Escalation Skills**
> Learn to defuse confrontations verbally to avoid physical altercations.
> Stay calm, speak clearly, and avoid provoking further aggression.

3. **Know When to Walk Away**
> Understand that safety often means avoiding unnecessary risks.
> Never let pride or ego push you into dangerous situations.

Real-Life Example: Defending Yourself and Staying Safe

During high school, I joined the military a decision that profoundly influenced my perspective on safety and self-defense. During basic training, I didn't just learn physical combat skills; I was taught the critical importance of situational awareness. This training instilled in me a heightened sense of vigilance, teaching me to assess potential threats and remain aware of my surroundings at all times. Such awareness is not just a military asset; it's a vital skill for everyday life, enabling individuals to navigate the world with confidence and preparedness.

One evening, while out with friends at a local pool hall I found myself in a situation that tested everything I'd learned. A group of intoxicated strangers began to escalate tensions, and the atmosphere quickly turned hostile. Relying on my training, I remained calm, assessed the situation, and prepared to act if necessary. Recognizing the potential danger, I reached for my licensed firearm not to intimidate, but to ensure I could protect myself and those around me. I drew the weapon responsibly, keeping it lowered but visible, and used verbal de-escalation techniques to diffuse the tension. My calm demeanor and readiness to act conveyed that I was in control, ultimately preventing the situation from spiraling into violence.

This experience reinforced the value of my military training and the importance of responsible self-defense. It's not about seeking confrontation but being prepared to protect oneself and others when necessary. Situational awareness and the ability to remain composed under pressure are crucial skills that can make all the difference in critical moments.

Self-defense training isn't exclusive to military personnel; it's a valuable resource for civilians as well. Such training emphasizes situational awareness, decision-making under stress, and conflict resolution tactics, empowering individuals to navigate challenging situations confidently. By investing in self-defense education, people can enhance their personal safety and contribute to a more secure community.

Adopting a mindset of vigilance and preparedness is essential in today's world. Whether through military experience or civilian self-defense training, the goal remains the same: to protect oneself and others responsibly. By sharing my experiences and emphasizing the importance of situational awareness, I hope to inspire others to take proactive steps toward their own safety and well-being.

Action Plan: Strengthening Your Safety and Defense

1. Enroll in a self-defense, martial arts, or boxing class.

2. Carry a safety tool, like pepper spray or a tactical flashlight, and learn how to use it effectively.

3. Review your home and online safety measures and make improvements where needed.

4. Create and practice an emergency plan for different scenarios.

5. Commit to staying alert and avoiding risky behaviors.

Closing Thought

Self-defense and safety are about empowering yourself to face the unpredictable with confidence and competence. By cultivating awareness, learning essential techniques, and adopting preventative measures, you can protect yourself and those you care about. Remember, a better man values life and takes responsibility for safeguarding it. Stay vigilant, stay prepared, and live boldly without fear.

"Let your heart serve as your compass and your mind the map; in the landscape of emotions, resilience lights the way."

INSPIRED BY VIKTOR FRANKL

Chapter

07:

Emotional Intelligence and Mental Resilience

Emotional intelligence (EI) and mental resilience are crucial traits for personal and professional growth. They help you understand your emotions, manage your reactions, and navigate relationships with empathy and clarity. Combined, these skills form the backbone of mental strength, enabling you to persevere through challenges, make sound decisions, and lead with confidence.

In this chapter, you'll learn how to enhance your emotional intelligence and develop the mental resilience needed to thrive under pressure and handle life's inevitable setbacks.

What Is Emotional Intelligence?

Emotional intelligence is the ability to recognize, understand, and manage your own emotions while also understanding and influencing the emotions of others.

Key Components of Emotional Intelligence

1. **Self-awareness:** Recognizing and understanding your emotions and how they affect your behavior.

2. **Self-Regulation:** Managing your emotions to stay in control and make rational decisions.

3. **Motivation:** Using emotional energy to pursue goals with determination and optimism.

4. **Empathy:** Understanding and sharing the feelings of others, fostering deeper connections.

5. **Social Skills:** Building and maintaining healthy relationships through effective communication and collaboration.

What Is Mental Resilience?

Mental resilience is your ability to adapt to adversity, bounce back from setbacks, and remain focused in the face of challenges.

Key Traits of Mental Resilience

➋ **Optimism:** Viewing challenges as opportunities to grow rather than as obstacles.

➋ **Self-Belief:** Trusting in your ability to overcome difficulties.

➋ **Emotional Stability:** Remaining calm and composed under pressure.

➋ **Adaptability:** Being flexible and open to change.

Step 1:

Building Self-Awareness

1. Reflect on Your Emotions

> Spend time identifying and labeling your emotions throughout the day.

> Use tools like journaling to document what triggers certain feelings and how you respond.

2. Identify Patterns

> Look for recurring emotional triggers or behaviors that affect your well-being or relationships.

> Awareness of these patterns is the first step toward change.

3. Mindfulness Practices

> Engage in mindfulness exercises like meditation or deep breathing to stay present and attuned to your emotions.

Mastering Self-Regulation

1. Pause Before Reacting

> When faced with an emotionally charged situation, take a moment to pause, breathe, and assess the best response.

2. Use Techniques to Calm Down

> Practice grounding exercises, such as focusing on your breath or counting to ten, to manage stress or anger.

> Remove yourself temporarily from situations that feel overwhelming.

3. Develop Emotional Flexibility

> Learn to accept emotions as they arise without judgment.

> Focus on problem-solving rather than dwelling on negative emotions.

Building Motivation

1. Set Meaningful Goals

> Align your goals with your values to stay intrinsically motivated.

> Break larger goals into smaller, manageable tasks to maintain momentum.

2. Maintain a Growth Mindset

> View failures as learning opportunities rather than setbacks.

> Celebrate progress and effort rather than just outcomes.

3. Develop Positive Habits

> Surround yourself with positive influences and adopt routines that support your mental and emotional well-being.

Practicing Empathy

1. **Active Listening**
> Give others your full attention, avoid interrupting, and show understanding through affirmations and clarifying questions.

2. **See from Their Perspective**
> Consider the emotions and experiences influencing someone's actions or decisions.

3. **Respond with Compassion**
> Avoid judgment and focus on offering support or constructive feedback.

Enhancing Social Skills

1. **Improve Communication**
> Use clear, concise language and maintain an open tone in conversations.
> Be assertive but respectful when expressing your needs or opinions.

2. **Build Rapport**
> Take a genuine interest in others by asking thoughtful questions and remembering details about their lives.

3. **Resolve Conflicts Effectively**
> Address conflicts calmly and collaboratively, seeking win-win solutions.
> Avoid escalating disagreements by focusing on common goals rather than differences.

Developing Mental Resilience

1. **Embrace Change**

> Practice adaptability by welcoming new challenges or shifting circumstances with an open mind.

2. **Strengthen Your Support System**

> Surround yourself with positive, encouraging people who can offer guidance and support.

> Build strong relationships by investing time and energy in those who matter most.

3. **Manage Stress**

> Use techniques like exercise, meditation, or creative outlets to process stress healthily.

> Create a balance between work and personal life to prevent burnout.

4. **Learn from Adversity**

> Reflect on past challenges to understand how you've grown and what you've learned.

> Use setbacks as motivation to keep moving forward.

Long-Term Emotional and Mental Health Practices

1. **Practice Gratitude**

> Write down three things you're grateful for each day to cultivate a positive outlook.

2. **Seek Professional Support When Needed**

> Don't hesitate to seek therapy or counseling if you're struggling with overwhelming emotions or stress.

3. **Stay Physically Active**

> Regular exercise is proven to boost mood, reduce stress, and improve mental clarity.

Real-Life Example: Balancing Emotions in Tough Times

Everyone desires a life filled with peace and longevity, but few are prepared for the moments when life unravels without warning. For me, that unraveling came with the loss of both of my fathers a profound grief compounded by financial hardship. It felt as though the foundation beneath me had crumbled, leaving me in a freefall of sorrow and uncertainty.

My biological father, Pastor Reid, underwent a heart transplant when I was in my early teens. Despite the odds, he was blessed to live beyond the expected lifespan of his new heart. He transitioned peacefully in the comfort of his home, a testament to his enduring faith and strength. Johnny, my second dad, passed away unexpectedly. After completing yard work, he suffered a fall that resulted in a head injury. Two days later, he was gone. The suddenness of his death was a shock that left me reeling. He was my best friend. Someone that I could talk to about any and everything that was on my mind.

In the depths of this turmoil, I faced a pivotal choice: to be consumed by despair or to find a way through it. I chose the latter, leaning heavily on my emotional intelligence and resilience. I turned to my faith, seeking solace and guidance through prayer, which became a daily ritual anchoring me amidst the chaos. Acknowledging my grief was the first step. I allowed myself to feel the pain without letting it dictate my actions. This self-awareness recognizing and naming my emotions was crucial. Instead of suppressing my feelings, I embraced them, understanding that they were a natural response to my losses. This approach aligns with the concept of emotional intelligence, which involves the ability to perceive, understand, and manage emotions effectively.

To regain a sense of control, I established small, daily routines. Budgeting became a way to navigate my financial struggles, and regular exercise helped me reconnect with my body and mind. These practices were not just tasks; they were affirmations of my agency and resilience. Meditation and self-reflection became tools for processing my grief. Through mindfulness, I learned to observe my thoughts without judgment, allowing me to respond rather than react to my emotions. This practice is supported by research indicating that mindfulness can enhance emotional regulation and resilience.

As I navigated this challenging period, I began to experience what psychologists refer to as post-traumatic growth a positive psychological change resulting from the struggle with highly challenging life circumstances. I developed a deeper appreciation for life, strengthened my relationships, and discovered personal strengths I hadn't recognized before. This growth didn't negate my pain but coexisted with it, illustrating that resilience isn't about bouncing back to a previous state but bouncing forward into a new, often stronger version of oneself.

Through this journey, I learned that emotional intelligence and resilience are not innate traits but skills that can be developed. By acknowledging emotions, seeking support, and establishing routines, I cultivated a resilience that not only helped me survive but also thrive. In sharing this experience, I hope to convey that while we cannot always control the challenges we face, we can choose how we respond to them. By developing emotional intelligence and resilience, we equip ourselves to navigate life's inevitable hardships with faith, grace, and strength.

Action Plan: Strengthening Emotional Intelligence and Resilience

1. Spend 5 minutes daily reflecting on your emotions and responses.

2. Practice mindfulness or meditation for at least 10 minutes a day.

3. Choose one relationship to nurture by actively listening and offering support.

4. Set one small, meaningful goal this week and take actionable steps toward it.

5. Identify one stress management technique to incorporate into your routine.

Closing Thought

Emotional intelligence and mental resilience are lifelong skills that empower you to navigate life with confidence, empathy, and strength. They enable you to connect with others, make sound decisions, and remain composed under pressure. By committing to self-awareness, empathy, and perseverance, you are not only becoming a better man but also creating a ripple effect of positivity and stability for those around you. Continue to grow, adapt, and inspire through your emotional strength and mental fortitude.

"Every heartfelt exchange is a chance to reshape our world, turning differences into shared paths of growth."

INSPIRED BY MARTIN LUTHER KING JR

08:

Building Stronger Bonds: Mastering Relationships and Conflict Resolution

Strong relationships are a cornerstone of a fulfilling life. Whether romantic, familial, professional, or platonic, the ability to connect with others, communicate effectively, and navigate conflicts with grace is essential to personal and relational growth. This chapter will guide you through building meaningful relationships, mastering the art of communication, and resolving conflicts with respect and empathy.

The Importance of Healthy Relationships

➡ **Emotional Support:** Meaningful relationships provide a foundation of support during challenges.

➡ **Personal Growth:** Healthy connections encourage self-reflection and development.

➡ **Fulfillment:** Deep, authentic bonds enhance life satisfaction and happiness.

Step 1:

Building Strong Relationships

1. **Establishing Trust**

> **Be reliable:** Follow through on commitments and show consistency in your actions.

> **Be honest:** Openly share your thoughts and feelings without deception or manipulation.

> **Respect boundaries:** Understand and honor the comfort levels and needs of others.

2. **Show Vulnerability**

> Open up about your feelings, fears, and dreams. Vulnerability fosters closeness and mutual understanding.

> Encourage others to do the same by creating a safe, nonjudgmental space.

3. **Invest Time and Effort**

> Prioritize your relationships by dedicating time to meaningful interactions.

> Show appreciation for the people in your life through small gestures of kindness.

4. **Embrace Diversity**

> Seek relationships with people from different backgrounds, perspectives, and experiences.

> Value differences as opportunities for growth and learning.

Step 2:

The Foundations of Effective Communication

1. **Active Listening**

> **Focus on the speaker:** Eliminate distractions and give your full attention.

> **Reflect and clarify:** Repeat back what you've heard to ensure understanding.

> **Validate emotions:** Acknowledge the speaker's feelings without dismissing or interrupting.

2. **Speak Clearly and Honestly**

> Use "I" statements to express your needs and emotions (e.g., "I feel upset when...").

> Avoid blaming or accusing language, which can escalate tension.

> Be concise and direct, ensuring your message is understood.

3. **Practice Nonverbal Communication**

> Maintain open and confident body language (e.g., eye contact, relaxed posture).

> Be mindful of your tone and facial expressions, as they can impact how your message is received.

4. **Adapt Your Communication Style**

> Understand that different people have different communication preferences.

> Adjust your approach to suit the individual and the context.

Step 3:

Conflict Resolution Strategies

Conflicts are inevitable in any relationship. The key is handling them constructively.

1. **Address Issues Promptly**

> Don't let resentment build by avoiding difficult conversations.

> Approach conflicts as soon as possible to prevent misunderstandings from growing.

2. **Maintain Emotional Control**

> Take a deep breath and pause before responding to emotional triggers.

> If needed, take a break to cool down before continuing the discussion.

3. **Focus on the Issue, Not the Person**

> Avoid personal attacks or bringing up past mistakes.

> Keep the conversation centered on the specific issue at hand.

4. **Use Collaborative Problem-Solving**

> Define the problem clearly and acknowledge each other's perspectives.

> Brainstorm solutions together and aim for compromises that benefit both parties.

5. **Apologize and Forgive**

> Take responsibility for your mistakes and offer sincere apologies.

> Be willing to forgive and move forward, letting go of grudges.

Strengthening Friendships

1. Be Present

> Make an effort to check in regularly and spend quality time together.

> Celebrate your friends' successes and offer support during tough times.

2. Communicate Openly

> Share your thoughts and feelings to deepen the connection.

> Be willing to give and receive constructive feedback.

3. Handle Disagreements Gracefully

> Approach conflicts with humility and a desire to preserve the friendship.

> Be willing to compromise and find a middle ground.

Professional Relationships and Networking

1. Show Professionalism

> Be punctual, respectful, and reliable in your interactions.

> Maintain a positive attitude and contribute constructively to team dynamics.

2. Build Genuine Connections

> Take an interest in colleagues beyond work-related topics.

> Offer help or mentorship to foster goodwill.

3. Handle Workplace Conflicts with Tact

> Address disagreements privately and professionally.

> Seek solutions that align with the team's goals and priorities.

Managing Toxic Relationships

Not all relationships are healthy, and recognizing when to set boundaries is crucial.

1. Identify Toxic Patterns

> Look for signs of manipulation, disrespect, or repeated negativity.

> Assess whether the relationship contributes to or detracts from your well-being.

2. Set Firm Boundaries

> Communicate your limits clearly and consistently.

> Be prepared to enforce boundaries if they are violated.

3. Know When to Let Go

> If a relationship is consistently harmful, consider distancing yourself or ending it altogether.

> Prioritize your mental health and emotional safety.

Step 8:

Navigating Loneliness & Finding Brotherhood

Loneliness is a silent struggle for many men, yet few openly discuss it. Finding a strong sense of brotherhood a community of supportive, like-minded men can provide emotional strength, personal growth, and lifelong friendships.

1. Understanding the Importance of Brotherhood

> **Emotional Support:** A strong group of friends can help you navigate life's challenges, from career struggles to personal hardships.

> **Accountability & Growth:** Surrounding yourself with motivated, disciplined men encourages you to stay on track with your goals.

> **A Sense of Belonging:** Brotherhood provides connection, reducing feelings of isolation and loneliness.

> **Skill-Sharing & Mentorship:** Learning from others' experiences can help you develop personally and professionally.

2. **How to Find & Build Brotherhood**

> Join Groups & Communities

> Seek out men's groups, sports teams, or hobby-based clubs.

> Attend networking events, religious gatherings, or leadership programs.

> Be Intentional About Relationships

> Invest time in friendships consistency builds strong bonds.

> Be open and vulnerable about your struggles and successes.

> Give as Much as You Take

> Brotherhood is about mutual support be a dependable friend.

> Offer encouragement, advice, and help when your friends need it.

> Seek Brotherhood in Different Areas of Life

> Have friends who challenge you intellectually, emotionally, and physically.

> Surround yourself with people who push you to be a better man.

3. **The Benefits of Finding Brotherhood**

> **Stronger Mental Health:** Reduces stress, anxiety, and depression by providing a reliable support system.

> **Increased Motivation & Drive:** Being around high-achieving men inspires personal growth.

> **Better Emotional Resilience:** Having a trusted group helps you navigate difficult times with confidence.

> **A Lasting Legacy:** Brotherhood fosters lifelong relationships that leave a positive impact on your life and future generations.

A man is only as strong as the community he builds around him. Brotherhood is not just about companionship it's about mutual growth, support, and becoming the best version of yourself.

Real-Life Example: Resolving Conflict to Strengthen a Relationship

We all reach a point where we've had enough a moment when emotions boil over, and we act before thinking. In middle school, I experienced such a moment with my close friend Shemar. What began as a minor disagreement escalated into a full-blown fistfight. Blood was everywhere, and if time could place you there you would think that we were two maniacs trying to kill each other. After the dust settled, I was left with a whirlwind of emotions: anger, guilt, and a deep sense of loss. Shemar wasn't just a friend; he was like a brother. The thought of losing our bond over a moment of rage was unbearable. I knew I had to make amends, but the path to reconciliation wasn't clear.

Finding the strength, I approached Shemar to talk. We sat down, and I listened truly listened to his perspective. I shared my feelings without placing blame, focusing instead on how much our friendship meant to me. Through this honest and open dialogue, we acknowledged our mistakes and the pain we caused each other. It wasn't easy, but our mutual respect and understanding paved the way for healing. This experience taught me the invaluable lesson that effective communication and conflict resolution can transform even the most strained relationships. By facing our issues head-on and engaging in heartfelt conversation, we not only salvaged our friendship but strengthened it. Nearly 20 years later, Shemar and I remain close friends a testament to the power of empathy, active listening, and the willingness to forgive.

In any relationship, conflicts are inevitable. However, it's our response to these conflicts that defines the strength and depth of our connections. By embracing vulnerability, practicing empathy, and committing to open communication, we can turn disagreements into opportunities for growth and deeper understanding. Remember, it's not about avoiding conflict but about navigating it with grace and integrity. Through these experiences, we not only become better friends but better individuals.

Action Plan: Enhancing Your Relationships

1. Identify one relationship to improve and take actionable steps to strengthen it.

2. Practice active listening in your next conversation by focusing entirely on the speaker.

3. Address a minor conflict using collaborative problem-solving.

4. Set a goal to check in regularly with close friends or family.

5. Evaluate any toxic relationships and consider setting boundaries or stepping away if needed.

Closing Thought

Healthy relationships are built on trust, communication, and mutual respect. By developing these skills, you can create deeper connections, resolve conflicts effectively, and foster a positive environment for growth and collaboration. Remember, a better man isn't perfect he is intentional, empathetic, and committed to cultivating relationships that enrich his life and the lives of others. Continue striving to be the kind of person others feel safe, valued, and respected around.

> *"Family is your first masterpiece nurture it with unwavering love, and watch your legacy bloom into timeless art."*

INSPIRED BY MAYA ANGELOU

Chapter

09:

The Power of Family: Nurturing Connections and Building a Legacy of Love

Family is often the foundation of our identity, shaping who we are and influencing how we navigate the world. Healthy family dynamics foster connection, understanding, and growth, while unhealthy dynamics can lead to conflict and strain. In this chapter, we'll explore the components of a strong family dynamic, strategies for improving communication, ways to manage conflicts, and how to take responsibility for your role within your family.

The Importance of Family

❯ **Support System:** Families provide emotional, financial, and moral support during life's challenges.

❯ **Growth and Identity:** Family relationships shape our self-esteem, values, and worldviews.

❯ **Legacy:** Positive family dynamics create a ripple effect, influencing future generations.

Step 1:

Understanding Your Family Dynamics

1. **Recognize Family Roles**

   ❯ Understand the roles each member plays (e.g., caretaker, peacemaker, leader) and how these impact relationships.

   ❯ Reflect on your role in the family and whether it fosters connection or conflict.

2. **Identify Strengths and Weaknesses**

   ❯ List the strengths of your family, such as unity, open communication, or shared traditions.

   ❯ Acknowledge areas for improvement, like unresolved conflicts or unhealthy communication patterns.

3. Acknowledge Family History

> Reflect on how your family's cultural background, traditions, and past experiences shape your dynamic.

> Consider how generational patterns may influence behaviors and interactions.

Step 2:

Improving Communication Within Your Family

1. Create Open Channels for Communication

> Encourage family members to share their thoughts and feelings without fear of judgment.

> Establish regular times for family discussions, such as weekly check-ins or family meetings.

2. Practice Listening

> Give family members your full attention when they're speaking.

> Validate their feelings by acknowledging their emotions and paraphrasing their concerns.

3. Avoid Assumptions

> Ask questions to clarify misunderstandings rather than assuming someone's intentions.

> Be transparent about your thoughts and feelings to prevent miscommunication.

Setting Boundaries

Healthy families respect each other's individuality and personal space.

1. **Define Personal Boundaries**
   > communicate your needs and limits to family members.
   > Respect the boundaries others set, even if they differ from your own.

2. **Avoid Overstepping**
   > Recognize when your actions or advice may come across as intrusive.
   > Allow family members to make their own decisions, even if you don't agree with them.

3. **Balance Togetherness and Independence**
   > Spend quality time together, but also support each other's need for personal space and self-growth.

Navigating Family Conflicts

Conflict is a natural part of family life, but it doesn't have to harm relationships.

1. **Address Issues Early**
   > Don't let resentment build by avoiding uncomfortable conversations.
   > Approach conflicts with the goal of resolution rather than blame.

2. **Stay Calm and Respectful**
   > Avoid yelling, name-calling, or using hurtful language.
   > If emotions are running high, take a break and revisit the conversation later.

3. **Seek Win-Win Solutions**

> Look for compromises that meet everyone's needs rather than trying to "win" the argument.

> Be willing to let go of minor grievances to focus on the bigger picture.

4. **Involve a Neutral Party When Necessary**

> For persistent or complex conflicts, consider family counseling or mediation.

> A third party can provide objective guidance and facilitate healthy communication.

Step 5:

Strengthening Family Bonds

1. **Create Traditions**

> Establish rituals that bring the family together, like Sunday dinners, holiday celebrations, or game nights.

> Traditions foster a sense of belonging and continuity.

2. **Spend Quality Time Together**

> Prioritize activities that everyone enjoys, such as outings, vacations, or hobbies.

> Focus on being present and engaged rather than distracted by technology.

3. **Show Appreciation**

> Regularly express gratitude for your family members' contributions and support.

> Small gestures, like a thank-you note or verbal acknowledgment, go a long way.

Parenting and Leadership in the Family

1. Lead by Example

> Model the behavior and values you want to see in your family, such as respect, kindness, and responsibility.

> Be consistent in your actions, as children and younger family members learn by observing.

2. Foster Emotional Safety

> Create an environment where family members feel safe expressing their emotions without fear of criticism.

> Teach emotional regulation by remaining calm during tense situations.

3. Encourage Independence

> Support children and younger family members in making their own choices and learning from mistakes.

> Balance guidance with allowing autonomy.

Healing and Repairing Broken Relationships

Sometimes, family relationships become strained due to past conflicts or misunderstandings.

1. Acknowledge the Pain

> Recognize the hurt feelings or actions that caused the rift.

> Validate the other person's experience without becoming defensive.

2. **Extend and Accept Apologies**
> Offer a sincere apology for your part in the conflict.
> Be open to accepting apologies from others, even if healing takes time.

3. **Rebuild Trust Gradually**
> Focus on small, positive interactions to restore the relationship.
> Be patient and consistent in showing that you value the connection.

Step 8:

Balancing Family Obligations and Personal Goals

1. **Manage Expectations**
> Communicate your personal goals and responsibilities to your family.
> Set realistic expectations for how much time and energy you can dedicate to family obligations.

2. **Prioritize Self-Care**
> Remember that you can't pour from an empty cup. Taking care of yourself enables you to show up fully for your family.

3. **Delegate Responsibilities**
> Share household tasks and responsibilities among family members.
> Encourage teamwork to lighten the load and foster collaboration.

Real-Life Example: Overcoming Family Challenges

We all reach moments in life that test the very core of our being. For me, that moment came with the passing of my father. His death not only left a void in our hearts but also unveiled deep-seated tensions within our family. Grief, with its unpredictable nature, brought misunderstandings to the surface, and despite our efforts to communicate and support one another, many disagreements remain unresolved. In the quiet that followed our shared sorrow, I found myself reflecting on the memories my father left behind the gentle reminders of his love, his unwavering strength, and the way his laughter could fill a room. These memories became my anchor, reminding me of the importance of family and the bonds that tie us together.

Navigating the complexities of grief and familial conflict has been a journey of introspection and resilience. I began by acknowledging my own emotions, allowing myself to feel the pain without letting it consume me. I also recognized the importance of open communication. While it hasn't been easy, I've made conscious efforts to reach out to my family members, to listen without judgment, and to express my feelings honestly. I hold onto hope that, in time, we can come together, communicate openly, and find healing. Losing my father taught me how precious family is. It reinforced the idea that, despite our differences, the love we share can be a unifying force. I pray that we can rebuild our bond before it's too late, honoring his legacy by nurturing the connections he valued so deeply.

Each day, I take small steps toward mending our broken ties, holding onto the belief that our shared past and the lessons he imparted can guide us back to one another. In the midst of unresolved conflicts, I nurture the hope that our future will be marked by understanding, forgiveness, and a renewed commitment to one another a future where the love for our father becomes the bridge that brings us home. I love them all dearly. This experience has taught me that the path to healing is not linear, but with patience, empathy, and a willingness to confront our pain, we can find our way back to each other. It's a journey worth undertaking, for the sake of our family and the legacy of love our father left behind.

Action Plan: Enhancing Your Family Dynamic

1. Schedule a family meeting to discuss how everyone can communicate more effectively.

2. Identify one family tradition to create or revive.

3. Write down three ways you can show appreciation to your family members this week.

4. Address a minor family conflict using the principles of calm communication and compromise.

5. Evaluate your boundaries and communicate them to your family.

Closing Thought

Family dynamics are complex, but they are also one of the most rewarding aspects of life. By fostering open communication, mutual respect, and strong connections, you can build a family environment that nurtures growth, understanding, and love. Remember, no family is perfect, but with effort and intention, you can create a dynamic where everyone feels valued, supported, and heard. A better man takes responsibility for his role in shaping and improving his family relationships, leaving a lasting legacy for generations to come.

"True wealth isn't just a number it's the discipline and vision that turn small savings into a legacy of abundance."

INSPIRED BY WARREN BUFFETT

Financial Responsibility and Wealth Building

Financial success is not just about earning money it's about managing it wisely, planning for the future, and building a legacy of wealth that provides security and opportunities. In this chapter, we'll dive into the principles of financial responsibility, strategies for saving and investing, and habits that promote long-term wealth.

The Importance of Financial Responsibility

➲ **Security:** Financial stability reduces stress and provides peace of mind.

➲ **Opportunity:** Wealth allows you to pursue goals, invest in yourself, and support others.

➲ **Legacy:** Responsible financial management ensures future generations benefit from your efforts.

Step 1:

Understanding Financial Responsibility

1. **Define Your Financial Goals**
   > Identify short-term goals (e.g., saving for a vacation, or paying off debt).
   > Establish long-term objectives (e.g., buying a home, retiring comfortably).
   > Prioritize goals based on your current financial situation and future aspirations.

2. **Create a Budget**
   > Track your income and expenses to understand where your money is going.
   > Use the 50/30/20 rule:
   > 50% for needs (rent, utilities, food).
   > 30% for wants (entertainment, dining out).
   > 20% for savings and debt repayment.
   > Regularly review and adjust your budget to stay aligned with your goals.

3. **Eliminate Debt**
> List all debts, including credit cards, loans, and mortgages.

> Focus on paying off high-interest debt first (e.g., credit card balances).

> Use strategies like Debt Snowball (paying off smallest debts first) or Debt Avalanche (tackling high-interest debts first).

Step 2:

Building Wealth Through Savings

1. **Establish an Emergency Fund**
> Aim to save 6-9 months of living expenses as life will only get more expensive.

> Keep this fund in a high-yield savings account for easy access.

2. **Automate Savings**
> Set up automatic transfers to your savings account each month.

> Treat your savings like a non-negotiable expense.

3. **Save for Major Life Goals**
> Create separate savings accounts for specific goals, such as buying a car, traveling, or education.

> Use tools like savings calculators to determine how much to set aside regularly.

Investing for the Future

1. **Understand the Basics of Investing**

> Learn about different types of investments, such as stocks, bonds, mutual funds, and real estate.

> Diversify your portfolio to minimize risk and maximize returns.

2. **Start Early**

> Take advantage of compound interest by starting to invest as early as possible.

> Even small contributions grow significantly over time.

3. **Utilize Retirement Accounts**

> Contribute to employer-sponsored plans like a 401(k), but only if your employer offers matching contributions.

> Consider opening an Individual Retirement Account (IRA) for additional tax-advantaged savings.

4. **Work with a Financial Advisor**

> Seek professional advice to create an investment strategy aligned with your goals.

> Regularly review your portfolio to ensure it stays on track.

Step 4:

Generating Additional Income Streams

1. **Explore Side Hustles**

> Identify skills or hobbies you can monetize, such as freelance work, teaching, or selling handmade products.

> Dedicate time each week to building your side hustle.

2. **Invest in Real Estate**
> Research opportunities to buy, rent, or flip properties.
> Consider real estate investment trusts (REITs) if direct property ownership isn't feasible.

3. **Build Passive Income**
> Look into options like dividend-paying stocks, peer-to-peer lending, or creating digital products.
> Focus on investments that generate income with minimal ongoing effort.

Step 5:

Developing Healthy Financial Habits

1. **Track Your Spending**
> Use apps or spreadsheets to monitor expenses and identify unnecessary costs.
> Review your financial activity monthly to stay accountable.

2. **Live Below Your Means**
> Avoid lifestyle inflation as your income grows.
> Prioritize saving and investing over excessive spending on luxuries.

3. **Avoid Impulse Purchases**
> Implement a "24-hour rule" before making non-essential purchases.
> Focus on needs over wants to maintain financial discipline.

4. **Practice Delayed Gratification**
> Save for larger purchases instead of using credit.
> Appreciate the rewards of patience and planning.

Protecting Your Wealth

1. Get Adequate Insurance

> Ensure you have health, life, auto, and home insurance to protect your assets.

> Review policies regularly to ensure they meet your current needs.

2. Plan for the Unexpected

> Create a will or trust to outline how your assets will be distributed after your death.

> Designate a power of attorney and healthcare proxies to manage decisions if you're unable to.

3. Monitor Your Credit Score

> Regularly check your credit report for accuracy.

> Maintain a good credit score by paying bills on time and keeping credit utilization low.

Step 7:

Teaching Financial Responsibility to Others

1. Lead by Example

> Show others the value of budgeting, saving, and investing through your actions.

> Share your financial successes and lessons learned.

2. Educate Your Family

> Teach children the importance of saving, budgeting, and making smart financial decisions.

> Encourage open discussions about money to reduce stigma and promote understanding.

3. **Support Financial Literacy**

> Recommend books, courses, or tools to help others improve their financial knowledge. Gift them this book!

> Mentor others who are just starting their financial journey.

Step 8:

Seek a Mentor

1. **Why a Financial Mentor Matters**

> A mentor can provide guidance, wisdom, and real-world experience that no book or course can fully replicate.

> Learning from someone who has successfully managed their finances helps you avoid common mistakes and fast-track your financial growth.

> A mentor can hold you accountable, ensuring you stay on track with your financial goals.

2. **How to Find the Right Financial Mentor**

> Look within your network successful family members, colleagues, or business professionals may be willing to offer guidance.

> Join financial communities, networking groups, or online forums where experienced individuals share their knowledge.

3. **How to Get the Most Out of a Mentorship**

> Come prepared with specific questions and goals.

> Apply what you learn and update your mentor on your progress.

> Offer value in return whether it's gratitude, referrals, or assistance in their endeavors.

Seeking a mentor is one of the most powerful steps in mastering financial responsibility. The right guidance can accelerate your success and help you avoid costly mistakes.

Real-Life Example: Transforming Financial Habits

We all aspire to achieve financial success, but the journey is often paved with hard lessons and pivotal moments that shape our understanding of money. For me, one such moment was the day I realized I had made a costly mistake by purchasing a 2013 Hyundai Sonata with a staggering 24% interest rate. At the time, I lacked financial literacy and didn't fully grasp the implications of such a high-interest loan. The situation worsened when the car became undrivable due to issues stemming from the dealership's service department. Without reliable transportation and burdened by a $15,600 debt to Navy Federal, I found myself in a financial quagmire. I was forced to pay for alternative transportation to get to work, stretching my already limited income even thinner.

This challenging period served as a wake-up call. Determined to change my circumstances, I immersed myself in learning about personal finance. I educated myself on budgeting, credit building, and money management. Over time, I paid off my debt, rebuilt my credit, and made more informed financial decisions. My efforts culminated in a significant milestone: making my first million dollars. The sense of accomplishment and empowerment I felt was indescribable. It wasn't just about the money; it was about the journey, the lessons learned, and the resilience developed along the way.

This experience reinforced the importance of financial literacy and being proactive in addressing financial challenges. It taught me that setbacks can be transformed into opportunities for growth and that with knowledge and determination, it's possible to overcome even the most daunting financial obstacles. Today, I continue to prioritize financial education and responsibility. I understand the value of making informed decisions and the impact they have on long-term financial well-being. My journey serves as a testament to the power of resilience and the transformative effect of financial literacy.

I later sued the dealership and in 2021, I joined a class-action lawsuit against Hyundai due to the issues with the engine in the Sonata. The lawsuit, known as the Hyundai Theta Engine Class Action Settlement, addressed defects in certain Hyundai vehicles, including the 2013 Sonata. The settlement was approved by the court, and eligible class members were entitled to compensation for their losses.

Action Plan: Improving Your Financial Responsibility

1. Create a detailed budget and track your expenses for the next 30 days.

2. Set up an emergency fund if you don't already have one.

3. Research and open a retirement account, if applicable.

4. Identify one side hustle or investment opportunity to pursue this year.

5. Review your insurance policies and credit report to ensure your assets are protected.

Closing Thought

Financial responsibility is essential for becoming a better man. By managing your money wisely, planning for the future, and building wealth, you create opportunities for yourself and those you care about. Remember, wealth is not just about material possessions it's about the freedom to live life on your terms and leave a positive legacy for others. Take small, consistent steps today to secure a financially responsible and prosperous future.

"*Love is like a timeless melody, where every act of faith and every vow of commitment forms a duet that resonates through every season of life.*"

INSPIRED BY RUMI AND PABLO NERUDA

Love, Commitment, and Partnership: Navigating Dating and Marriage

Relationships are one of life's most profound experiences, offering opportunities for connection, growth, and mutual support. However, creating a healthy romantic relationship requires effort, self-awareness, and a commitment to your partner's well-being. In this chapter, we'll explore how to navigate dating with purpose, cultivate a meaningful partnership, and build a strong foundation for a lasting marriage.

The Role of Relationships in Personal Growth

- ❯ **Emotional Fulfillment:** A healthy partnership provides love, care, and companionship.

- ❯ **Mutual Support:** Couples grow stronger by supporting each other's dreams and navigating challenges together.

- ❯ **Self-Discovery:** Relationships help you understand yourself better, including your needs, boundaries, and capacity to love.

Step 1:

Purposeful Dating

1. **Clarify Your Intentions**
   > Decide what you're looking for in a relationship (e.g., casual dating, long-term partnership).

   > Reflect on your non-negotiables, such as shared values, life goals, or emotional compatibility.

2. **Work on Yourself First**
   > Before seeking a partner, ensure you are emotionally and mentally healthy.

   > Develop self-confidence, clear goals, and independence to avoid relying on a partner to "complete" you.

3. **Look in the Right Places**

> Seek out like-minded individuals in environments that align with your values, such as community events, hobbies, or professional networks.

> Avoid rushing into relationships purely for convenience or out of fear of being alone.

4. **Prioritize Communication Early**

> Be open and honest about your expectations and goals.

> Practice active listening to understand your potential partner's needs and perspectives.

Step 2:

Building a Strong Foundation

1. **Understand Compatibility**

> Evaluate your compatibility in key areas such as values, lifestyle, and long-term goals.

> Recognize the difference between superficial attraction and deep emotional connection.

2. **Develop Emotional Intimacy**

> Share your vulnerabilities, fears, and dreams to foster trust and closeness.

> Show empathy by validating your partner's emotions and experiences.

3. **Cultivate Respect and Kindness**

> Treat your partner with respect, even during disagreements.

> Appreciate their individuality and avoid trying to change them to meet your expectations.

4. **Learn to Compromise**

> Accept that no one is perfect, and relationships require give-and-take.

> Focus on finding solutions that meet both your needs rather than "winning" arguments.

The Art of Communication in Relationships

1. Practice Effective Communication

> Use "I" statements to express your feelings without blaming (e.g., "I feel hurt when...").

> Listen actively, without interrupting or formulating a response while your partner is speaking.

2. Avoid Toxic Patterns

> Steer clear of criticism, defensiveness, stonewalling, and contempt.

> Address conflicts calmly and focus on resolving the issue rather than attacking your partner.

3. Be Transparent

> Share your thoughts, feelings, and concerns openly to avoid misunderstandings.

> Build trust by being consistent in your words and actions.

Navigating Marriage

1. Shift from "Me" to "We"

> Understand that marriage is a partnership where decisions affect both individuals.

> Foster teamwork in managing finances, household responsibilities, and family matters.

2. Keep the Romance Alive

> Regularly prioritize quality time together, even amidst busy schedules.

> Surprise your partner with small gestures of love, like notes, gifts, or planned dates.

3. **Plan for the Future Together**
> Discuss your shared goals, such as having children, buying a home, or pursuing career aspirations.
> Be proactive in creating a financial plan that ensures long-term stability.

4. **Embrace Change**
> Recognize that both individuals will grow and evolve.
> Adapt to changes with an open mind and commitment to strengthening your bond.

Step 5:

Managing Conflict in Relationships

1. **Address Problems Early**
> Don't let issues fester small conflicts can grow into major problems if left unaddressed.
> Approach disagreements with a problem-solving mindset.

2. **Learn to Apologize**
> Take accountability for your mistakes and offer genuine apologies.
> Avoid excuses or minimizing your partner's feelings.

3. **Resolve Conflict Productively**
> Focus on the issue at hand without bringing up past grievances.
> Take breaks during heated arguments to regain perspective before continuing the discussion.

4. **Know When to Seek Help**
> If conflicts persist, consider couples counseling to gain professional guidance.
> Therapy can provide tools to improve communication and rebuild trust.

5. **Validating Feelings**

> Recognize that your partner's emotions are real and important, even if you see the situation differently.

> Listen actively and without judgment, allowing them to express their feelings fully.

> Validate their feelings by acknowledging their perspective and the impact of the conflict on them.

> Use empathetic language to affirm that their feelings are valid. Phrases like "I can see why you feel that way" or "Your feelings matter to me" can soften tension and create a supportive dialogue.

> Ask clarifying questions such as, "Can you tell me more about what made you feel this way?" This not only shows that you care but also deepens your understanding of their perspective.

> Remain patient and avoid defensiveness, even if you feel misunderstood. Sometimes a pause, a deep breath, and a calm acknowledgment like "I hear you" can prevent further escalation and pave the way for resolution.

> Reinforce your commitment to their well-being by expressing that you are there to support them, and that their emotional experience is a priority in your relationship. This can build trust and promote a more empathetic connection during conflicts.

Step 6:

Maintaining Individuality in a Partnership

1. **Nurture Your Interests**

> Pursue hobbies, friendships, and personal growth outside the relationship.

> Encourage your partner to do the same to maintain balance and independence.

2. **Avoid Codependency**

> While it's important to rely on your partner, maintain your sense of self and independence.

> Set healthy boundaries to ensure mutual respect and autonomy.

Preparing for the Challenges of Marriage

1. **Financial Stress**

> Be transparent about finances, including debts, spending habits, and financial goals.

> Create a budget together to avoid misunderstandings about money.

2. **Family Dynamics**

> Set boundaries with extended family members to protect your relationship.

> Work as a team to navigate differences in family expectations or traditions.

3. **Maintaining Intimacy**

> Prioritize physical and emotional intimacy to keep your connection strong.

> Be proactive about addressing any challenges in your sex life or emotional closeness.

4. **Handling Life's Curveballs**

> Approach challenges, such as job loss or health issues, with a united front.

> Lean on each other for support and focus on solutions rather than blame.

Reassurance in a Relationship

1. **Why Reassurance is Important**

> **Builds Trust and Security:** Regular reassurance helps your partner feel valued and secure in the relationship, reducing feelings of doubt or insecurity.

> **Strengthens Emotional Connection:** Verbal affirmations, physical affection, and consistent actions convey commitment and love, deepening the bond between partners.

> **Fosters Open Communication:** When both partners feel emotionally supported, it encourages honest and open conversations about needs, concerns, and future goals.

2. **How Reassurance is Beneficial**

> **Reduces Anxiety:** Small gestures of reassurance, such as saying "I love you" or expressing appreciation, can ease anxiety and help your partner feel safe.

> **Encourages Vulnerability:** Reassurance creates a safe space for both partners to share their fears, dreams, and emotions without judgment.

> **Prevents Misunderstandings:** A habit of reassurance helps clarify intentions and reduces the likelihood of misinterpreting each other's actions or words.

> **Increases Relationship Satisfaction:** Regularly showing care and commitment fosters feelings of appreciation and satisfaction, contributing to a healthier and happier partnership.

Practical Ways to Reassure Your Partner

- **Use words of affirmation regularly:** Compliment your partner, acknowledge their efforts, and express gratitude.

- **Be physically affectionate:** Small gestures like holding hands, hugging, or a quick kiss can convey reassurance.

- **Show up consistently:** Follow through on promises and be present in moments of need.

- **Listen actively:** Pay attention to your partner's concerns and validate their feelings without dismissing or interrupting them.

- **Offer encouragement:** Cheer them on in their endeavors and celebrate their achievements.

Watch Your Tone

1. **Why Watching Your Tone is Important**

> **It's Not Always What You Say, but How You Say It:** The way words are delivered often carries more weight than the words themselves. Tone can amplify or diminish the message being communicated.

> **Prevents Misunderstandings:** A harsh or dismissive tone can lead to misinterpretation of intentions, even if the words are not meant to hurt.

> **Demonstrates Respect:** Speaking with a calm and respectful tone shows consideration for your partner's feelings, fostering mutual respect in the relationship.

> **Encourages Healthy Communication:** A gentle and understanding tone creates a safe environment for open and constructive dialogue.

2. **How Watching Your Tone is Beneficial**

> **Reduces Conflicts:** Using a calm and even tone can prevent arguments from escalating and help resolve issues more effectively.

> **Promotes Empathy:** A kind and supportive tone shows that you care about your partner's emotions, deepening emotional intimacy.

> **Builds Trust:** Consistently using a thoughtful tone reassures your partner that you value them, even during disagreements.

> **Strengthens Connection:** Positive communication habits, including a mindful tone, help maintain harmony and deepen the bond between partners.

3. **Practical Ways to Watch Your Tone**

> **Pause Before Responding:** Take a moment to reflect before speaking, especially in heated situations, to ensure your tone aligns with your intent.

> **Be Mindful of Volume:** Avoid raising your voice unnecessarily, as it can come across as aggressive or intimidating.

> **Choose Words Carefully:** Use kind, supportive, and affirming language to convey your message effectively.

- > **Pay Attention to Nonverbal Cues:** Facial expressions, body language, and voice inflection can all influence how your tone is perceived.

- > **Practice Active Listening:** Respond with empathy and validation to show your partner that you genuinely care about their perspective.

Watching your tone ensures that communication strengthens the relationship rather than creating distance or misunderstanding. The tone makes the music.

Step 8:

Defining Masculinity

In relationships, understanding and embracing a healthy form of masculinity is essential for fostering love, commitment, and partnership. True masculinity is not about dominance or emotional suppression but about strength, responsibility, and emotional intelligence.

What is Healthy Masculinity in a Relationship?

- → Strength Through Vulnerability – Being emotionally open does not make a man weak; it builds deeper intimacy and trust.

- → Leadership with Partnership – Leading in a relationship doesn't mean control it means guiding with love, support, and collaboration.

- → Providing Beyond Finances – True provision includes emotional security, stability, and being a source of comfort.

- → Respecting Boundaries – A strong man understands consent, emotional space, and the importance of mutual respect.

The Importance of Defining Masculinity in Love & Commitment

➡ Helps men show up fully in relationships without fear of being seen as "too emotional" or "not strong enough."

➡ Promotes balance allowing men to protect and provide while also nurturing and supporting.

➡ Encourages men to be present, engaged partners rather than emotionally distant figures.

Benefits of Embracing a Healthy Masculine Role in Relationships

1. Stronger Emotional Connection – Being confident in your masculinity allows you to love without fear or ego.

2. Increased Mutual Respect – A man who leads with integrity and care earns his partner's trust and admiration.

3. Better Conflict Resolution – Understanding that masculinity isn't about aggression but about control, patience, and wisdom.

4. Greater Relationship Satisfaction – When both partners embrace their strengths, the relationship thrives in harmony.

How to Define and Embrace Your Masculinity in Relationships

➡ Understand That Strength Includes Softness – You can be strong while also being kind, compassionate, and emotionally aware.

➡ Lead With Integrity – Keep your word, be honest, and take responsibility for your actions.

➡ Be a Protector, Not a Controller – Protection means providing safety and security, not restricting freedom.

➡ Embrace Growth and Adaptability – Healthy masculinity evolves, allowing you to become a better partner over time.

Defining masculinity in a relationship is about being a man who is strong, loving, responsible, and emotionally aware. The most attractive and respected men are those who confidently embrace their masculinity without fear of growth, change, or vulnerability.

Real-Life Example: The Dating Journey

Love is a synchronizer of hearts. We all yearn to find love and build meaningful connections, but the path is often fraught with unexpected challenges. At the beginning of 2024, I faced one of the most profound betrayals of my life. The woman I had been dating for several months, someone I deeply loved and trusted, had stolen $62,400 from me. The shock and betrayal were overwhelming, threatening to shatter my faith in love and trust. In the immediate aftermath, emotions surged anger, hurt, disbelief. Friends and family offered a cacophony of advice, some urging retaliation, others suggesting legal action. But amidst the turmoil, I realized that reacting impulsively would only compound the damage. I needed to anchor myself, to find clarity amidst the chaos.

Drawing upon the principles of emotional intelligence, I chose a path of introspection and restraint. I meditated, seeking clarity and understanding. Rather than confronting her with hostility, I extended an opportunity for her to return the money without conflict. To this day, she still owes $32,400. But more importantly, I preserved my integrity and peace of mind. This experience could have easily led me down a path of bitterness and mistrust. I could have allowed it to taint my view of relationships, to build walls around my heart. But I chose differently. I recognized that one person's actions should not dictate my capacity to love and trust. Each interaction, each relationship, is a new opportunity a chance to learn, to grow, and to connect on a deeper level.

Navigating the dating world as a single man has its challenges misunderstandings, mismatched expectations, moments of self-doubt. But through these experiences, I've learned the importance of clear communication, setting boundaries, and understanding both my needs and those of my partner. I've come to appreciate that vulnerability is not a weakness, but a strength a testament to one's courage to love despite past hurts. Embracing emotional intelligence in relationships means being self-aware, managing our emotions, and empathizing with our partners. It's about recognizing our triggers, communicating openly, and building trust through consistent actions. By cultivating these skills, we not only enhance our relationships but also foster personal growth.

In sharing this chapter of my life, I hope to inspire others to approach love and relationships with both heart and wisdom. To understand that while betrayal can wound deeply, it doesn't have to define our future. With emotional intelligence as our guide, we can navigate the complexities of love, heal from past wounds, and build partnerships rooted in trust, respect, and genuine connection.

Action Plan: Enhancing Your Relationship

1. Write down your non-negotiables and values in a partner, then evaluate how these align with your current or future relationship.

2. Schedule a date night or meaningful activity with your partner this week.

3. Identify one area of communication to improve and practice active listening during your next conversation.

4. Discuss long-term goals with your partner, such as financial planning or family aspirations.

5. Address a minor conflict constructively, focusing on resolution rather than blame.

Closing Thought

A fulfilling relationship or marriage isn't something that happens by chance it's built through intentional effort, respect, and a commitment to growth. Love is not only an emotion but also a series of actions that foster trust, connection, and mutual support. By approaching dating and marriage with purpose and care, you can create a partnership that enriches your life and serves as a foundation for personal and shared success. However, the term "happy wife, happy life" oversimplifies relationships, placing all the focus on one partner's happiness while neglecting the importance of mutual fulfillment. True partnership thrives on equal investment, where both individuals feel valued, heard, and supported in building a lasting bond. In the end, the key to a thriving relationship is striving for mutual happiness, where both partners grow and thrive together. Happy spouses mean happy houses.

"*Every hug plants a seed of love; listen deeply, guide gently, and love unconditionally, and watch your child's heart bloom into a garden of hope.*"

INSPIRED BY DR. BENJAMIN SPOCK

Chapter

12:

Nurturing Hearts: Becoming the Parent Your Children Deserve

Parenting is one of the most impactful roles you'll ever have. It's about more than providing for your children; it's about shaping their character, building their confidence, and guiding them to become responsible, kind, and independent individuals. This chapter will explore the core principles of effective parenting, including creating a nurturing environment, leading by example, and preparing your children to thrive in the world.

The Role of a Parent in a Child's Life

◉ **Modeling Behavior:** Children learn more from what you do than what you say.

◉ **Providing Stability:** A stable home offers children a sense of security and belonging.

◉ **Encouraging Independence:** Your ultimate goal is to raise children who can navigate life confidently and responsibly.

Step 1:

Building a Foundation of Love and Trust

1. **Create a Safe Emotional Environment**

> Be a source of unconditional love and support.

> Encourage open communication by being approachable and non-judgmental.

> Validate your child's feelings and teach them how to manage emotions constructively.

2. **Be Consistent**

> Establish clear rules and expectations for behavior.

> Follow through with both rewards and consequences to build trust and accountability.

3. Spend Quality Time Together

> Dedicate time to bond with your child through shared activities, conversations, or traditions.

> Practice active listening to show your child they are valued and understood.

Step 2:

Leading by Example

1. Demonstrate Integrity

> Show honesty, kindness, and respect in your daily interactions.

> Admit your mistakes and take accountability to teach humility and self-awareness.

2. Practice Self-Control

> Manage your own emotions and reactions, especially in challenging situations.

> Avoid yelling or reacting impulsively, as children model their emotional regulation on yours.

3. Prioritize Growth

> Show your commitment to personal growth, whether through learning new skills, pursuing goals, or improving relationships.

> Inspire your children by sharing what you've learned from challenges and successes.

Step 3:

Teaching Life Lessons

1. **Instill Core Values**
> Teach values like empathy, gratitude, and responsibility through everyday interactions.
> Reinforce these values by pointing out examples in your child's behavior or stories and media.

2. **Teach Financial Literacy**
> Start age-appropriate lessons about money, saving, and budgeting.
> Encourage them to earn their own money through chores, small jobs, or entrepreneurial efforts.

3. **Encourage Problem-Solving**
> Allow your child to face age-appropriate challenges and solve problems independently.
> Offer guidance without taking over, fostering their confidence and critical thinking skills.

Step 4:

Encouraging Independence

1. **Allow Room for Mistakes**
> Let your child make mistakes and learn from them in a safe environment.
> Focus on the lesson rather than punishing the failure.

2. **Foster Self-Reliance**
> Assign age-appropriate responsibilities, such as chores or decision-making.
> Teach them how to set and achieve goals, emphasizing the value of perseverance.

3. Promote a Growth Mindset

> Encourage your child to view challenges as opportunities to grow.

> Praise effort and improvement rather than just results to build resilience.

Step 5:

Balancing Discipline and Compassion

1. Set Clear Boundaries

> Use consistent, fair rules to provide structure and predictability.

> Communicate the reasoning behind rules so your child understands their purpose.

2. Use Positive Discipline

> Focus on teaching rather than punishing.

> Redirect negative behavior with constructive alternatives and reward good behavior to reinforce it.

3. Manage Conflict Constructively

> Approach disagreements calmly and listen to your child's perspective.

> Collaborate on solutions, teaching them negotiation and compromise skills.

Step 6:

Preparing Your Child for the World

1. Teach Social Skills

> Help your child build healthy relationships by teaching respect, empathy, and communication.

> Model how to handle conflicts and maintain boundaries.

2. **Equip Them with Practical Skills**
> Teach essential life skills such as cooking, cleaning, time management, and financial planning.

> Prepare them for independence by gradually giving them more responsibilities.

3. **Encourage Lifelong Learning**
> Promote curiosity by exposing your child to new ideas, cultures, and experiences.

> Support their interests and passions, no matter how different they are from your own.

Step 7:

Nurturing Your Parent-Child Bond Over Time

1. **Adapt as They Grow**
> Recognize that your parenting approach will need to evolve as your child's needs change.

> Stay involved in their life without being overbearing, respecting their independence.

2. **Celebrate Their Achievements**
> Acknowledge milestones and successes, no matter how small, to build their confidence.

> Celebrate their uniqueness and encourage them to embrace who they are.

3. **Be Present**
> Prioritize moments with your child, even amidst the busyness of life.

> Create rituals, like family dinners or weekly check-ins, to stay connected.

Effective Co-Parenting

Co-parenting is essential for providing a stable, supportive environment for children, even when parents are no longer together. Effective co-parenting ensures that children receive love, guidance, and consistency from both parents, which positively impacts their emotional and psychological well-being.

1. **Prioritize the Child's Well-Being**

> Always make decisions based on what is best for your child, rather than personal differences.

> Keep a united front on major parenting decisions to avoid confusion.

> Encourage a positive relationship between your child and the other parent.

2. **Maintain Respectful Communication**

> Speak to and about the other parent with respect, especially in front of your child.

> Keep conversations focused on the child's needs and avoid rehashing past conflicts.

> Use a neutral communication method if necessary (email, texts, or co-parenting apps).

3. **Create a Consistent Parenting Plan**

> Establish clear rules and expectations across both households for stability.

> Agree on a schedule that prioritizes your child's routine and well-being.

> Be flexible when changes are needed while maintaining fairness.

4. **Avoid Using Children as Messengers**

> Never put your child in the middle of adult conflicts or make them relay messages.

> Handle discussions about schedules, responsibilities, and concerns directly with the other parent.

5. **Support Each Other's Roles as Parents**

> Acknowledge and appreciate the other parent's contributions.

> Encourage your child to respect and value both parents.

> Avoid undermining the other parent's authority in front of the child.

6. **Handle Disagreements Maturely**

> Disagreements should be handled privately and calmly, without involving the child.

> If conflicts arise, focus on finding solutions rather than placing blame.

> Consider mediation or counseling if co-parenting struggles become difficult to resolve.

Importance & Benefits of Effective Co-Parenting

> **Emotional Stability for the Child:** Children thrive in environments where they feel safe and supported by both parents.

> **Consistent Discipline and Guidance:** Aligning parenting approaches helps children develop respect for boundaries.

> **Stronger Parent-Child Bonds:** Children benefit from having meaningful relationships with both parents.

> **Less Stress and Anxiety:** A peaceful co-parenting relationship reduces stress for both the child and the parents.

> **Positive Role Modeling:** Children learn how to handle relationships, communication, and conflict resolution by observing their parents.

Effective co-parenting isn't about being perfect it's about being intentional, respectful, and child-focused. By working together, even in separate households, both parents can ensure their child grows up feeling loved, secure, and supported.

Real-Life Example: A Parent's Journey

We all have heroes in our lives people whose tenacity shape us into who we are. For me, that hero is my mother. Her journey is a testament to resilience, transformation, and the boundless depths of a mother's love. Imagine raising seven children while battling homelessness and addiction. It's a scenario that would break many, but my mother faced it head-on. There were nights when we had no roof over our heads, days when uncertainty loomed large, and moments when despair threatened to consume us. Yet, through it all, she remained steadfast, determined to provide a better life for her children.

Her struggles were not just external. She grappled with personal demons alcoholism and smoking that added to the weight she carried. But one day, seemingly out of nowhere, she made a decision that would change our lives forever. She chose to stop drinking and smoking entirely, embarking on a journey of self-healing and transformation. Her battles didn't end there. She faced cancer with the same courage and determination, fighting through it without complaint. Through her strength and perseverance, she became a more present and loving parent. Today, she's not just my mother; she's my best friend. We talk every day, sharing our lives, our dreams, and our love.

Her journey has taught me invaluable lessons about parenting, love, and the power of determination. She showed me that no matter how dire the circumstances, it's possible to rise above them. She taught me how to navigate the world with integrity, compassion, and strength. Her unwavering dedication to her children, despite the absence of a supportive village at times, is a testament to her indomitable spirit. In a society where single mothers often face insurmountable challenges, my mother's story stands as a beacon of hope. Her transformation is a reminder that with love, determination, and willpower, we can overcome even the most daunting obstacles. She is, without a doubt, the best mother anyone could ask for. That's my big baby!

I use my mother's testimony as an example of how, by embracing the same principles of resilience, love, and unwavering commitment, a man can become the father his children deserve. Her life taught me that being a parent isn't about perfection it's about presence. It's about showing up, even when the odds are stacked against you. It's about making hard choices, sacrificing comfort, and pushing through personal battles so your children have a chance at something better.

As men, we often think strength is about stoicism or control. But my mother showed me that true strength is vulnerability, humility, and relentless love. She didn't have a manual, but she had a vision and that vision was us. So, to every father reading this: you don't need to be flawless. You need to be faithful. Faithful to your role, to your growth, and to the promise you made spoken or unspoken to be the man your children can count on. Let your children see you strive, stumble, and stand back up. Let them witness your evolution. Because in doing so, you're not just raising them you're raising yourself, and that's the kind of legacy that lasts. As of yesterday my mother graduated college at the age of 61.

Action Plan: Becoming a Better Parent

1. Identify one area where you want to improve as a parent (e.g., communication, discipline, quality time).

2. Set aside 30 minutes daily to spend one-on-one with your child, free from distractions.

3. Create a list of core values you want to instill in your child and brainstorm ways to teach them.

4. Reflect on your behaviors are you modeling the values and habits you want your child to adopt?

5. Celebrate one achievement, big or small, with your child this week to show your support and pride.

Closing Thought

Parenting is not about being perfect it's about being present, intentional, and loving. By striving to become the parent your child deserves, you are shaping the future not just for them, but for the world they will influence. Remember, the most meaningful legacy you can leave is the love, wisdom, and values you impart to your children. Let every action and decision reflect the kind of parent you aspire to be.

"Dive into the quiet depths of your soul; there, amid the stillness, you'll discover the peace that transforms chaos into clarity."

INSPIRED BY LAO TZU

Chapter

13:

The Path Within: Cultivating Spiritual Growth and Inner Peace

I n a world filled with distractions and chaos, cultivating spiritual growth and inner peace is essential for achieving balance and fulfillment. This chapter explores the journey of self-discovery, mindfulness, and connection to something greater than oneself. It's about finding clarity and purpose in life while fostering harmony within your mind, body, and soul.

Understanding Spiritual Growth and Inner Peace

❯ **Defining Spiritual Growth:** The process of deepening your connection with yourself, others, and the world around you. It doesn't have to be tied to religion but is often about purpose and meaning.

❯ **The Role of Inner Peace:** Inner peace allows you to remain calm and grounded, even in difficult circumstances, enabling better decision-making and relationships.

❯ **Why It Matters:** A strong sense of spirituality and inner calm improves mental health, reduces stress, and provides clarity in life's challenges.

Step 1:

Self-Reflection and Awareness

1. **Practice Daily Introspection**

> Set aside time to reflect on your thoughts, feelings, and actions each day.

> Ask yourself questions like: What did I do well today? What could I improve?

2. **Identify Your Values and Beliefs**

> Write down your core values what truly matters to you.

> Examine whether your daily actions align with those values.

3. **Embrace Vulnerability**

> Accept your imperfections and see them as opportunities for growth.

> Let go of the need for constant control and perfection.

Practicing Mindfulness

1. Live in the Present Moment

> Avoid dwelling on the past or worrying about the future.

> Engage fully in your current activities, whether it's eating, working, or spending time with loved ones.

2. Start a Mindfulness Practice

> Try techniques such as meditation, deep breathing, or yoga to cultivate focus and calmness.

> Begin with 5-10 minutes a day, gradually increasing as you become comfortable.

3. Develop Gratitude

> Keep a gratitude journal where you list three things you're thankful for each day.

> Gratitude shifts your focus from what's lacking to what you already have.

Step 3:

Connecting with Something Greater

1. Explore Spiritual Practices

> Engage in practices that resonate with you, such as prayer, meditation, or reading spiritual texts.

> Attend gatherings, such as religious services, meditation retreats, or nature walks, to foster a sense of community.

2. **Build a Connection with Nature**

> Spend time outdoors to feel grounded and connected to the natural world.

> Activities like hiking, gardening, or simply sitting under a tree can bring peace and perspective.

3. **Seek Meaning and Purpose**

> Identify what gives your life meaning whether it's helping others, creating art, or pursuing knowledge.

> Dedicate time and energy to these pursuits, as they bring fulfillment and alignment with your higher self.

Step 4:

Letting Go of Negativity

1. **Release Resentments**

> Holding onto anger or grudges only harms you. Practice forgiveness to lighten your emotional burden.

> Forgiveness doesn't mean excusing bad behavior but freeing yourself from its hold on your mind.

2. **Overcome Fear and Anxiety**

> Face your fears head-on and challenge negative thought patterns.

> Use calming techniques like visualization or breathing exercises to reduce anxiety.

3. **Declutter Your Mind and Life**

> Remove toxic influences, such as negative relationships or habits.

> Simplify your life by focusing on what truly matters, reducing distractions, and organizing your environment.

Step 5:

Cultivating Compassion and Kindness

1. Practice Empathy

> Put yourself in others' shoes to understand their perspective.

> Approach everyone with kindness, regardless of their attitude or behavior.

2. Serve Others

> Volunteer your time or resources to help those in need.

> Acts of service not only benefit others but also bring a sense of purpose and joy.

3. Practice Self-Compassion

> Treat yourself with the same kindness you would offer to a close friend.

> Accept your flaws and failures without judgment or self-criticism.

Step 6:

Building Daily Habits for Inner Peace

1. Create a Morning Routine

> Begin each day with practices that set a calm and positive tone, such as meditation, journaling, or stretching.

> Avoid jumping straight into emails or social media, which can add stress.

2. End Your Day with Reflection

> Before bed, reflect on what you're grateful for and what you learned during the day.

> Use this time to release any lingering stress or worries.

3. **Establish Boundaries**

> Protect your peace by saying no to unnecessary commitments or toxic people.

> Prioritize activities and relationships that bring you joy and fulfillment.

Step 7:

Embracing the Journey

1. **Accept That Growth Takes Time**

> Spiritual growth and inner peace are lifelong journeys, not destinations.

> Celebrate small victories and be patient with setbacks.

2. **Stay Open to New Experiences**

> Be willing to explore new practices, beliefs, and perspectives as you grow.

> Allow life's challenges to teach you resilience and wisdom.

3. **Honing Faith in the Process**

> Trust that everything in life happens for a reason, even if it's not immediately clear.

> Focus on staying present and doing your best, knowing that clarity will come with time.

Real-Life Example: A Journey to Inner Peace

Even though life has its challenges, I've come to see them not as roadblocks but as stepping stones that have shaped me to who i am today. Greatness isn't always an upward spiral. There was a time when stress and self-doubt weighed heavily on me, especially after the loss of my father's. I felt disconnected and unsure of how to move forward. In search of peace, I turned inward, prioritizing mindfulness and spirituality. Daily meditation became my sanctuary, offering moments of clarity in the midst of the storm. Spending time alone allowed me to reflect deeply and reconnect with what truly brought me joy.

One of the most profound shifts in my journey was embracing faith not just as a concept, but as a daily practice. I began to lean not on my own understanding, but on a higher power, trusting that even in my darkest moments, a path would be illuminated. This surrender wasn't about giving up control; it was about acknowledging that I didn't have to bear the weight of the world alone. Through this spiritual lens, I started to see challenges not as insurmountable obstacles, but as opportunities for growth and transformation. Each setback became a lesson, each hardship a stepping stone towards a more grounded and purposeful existence. I realized that no matter one's religious background or beliefs, we all have an intrinsic purpose on this earth a unique contribution that only we can make.

This journey inward didn't just heal my wounds; it awakened a deeper understanding of my place in the world. I found that by nurturing my spirit, I could better serve others, not from a place of obligation, but from genuine compassion and empathy. In embracing faith and inner peace, I discovered a wellspring of strength and resilience that continues to guide me through life's uncertainties. Remember, regardless of where you come from or what you've faced, your life holds immense value. By turning inward and connecting with your spiritual essence, you can uncover a sense of purpose and peace that transcends circumstances. You matter, and your journey towards inner harmony can inspire and uplift not only yourself but those around you.

Action Plan:
Cultivating Your Spiritual Growth

1. Dedicate 10 minutes daily to mindfulness or meditation.

2. Write down your core values and reflect on how you can live in alignment with them.

3. Identify one source of negativity in your life and take steps to address or eliminate it.

4. Plan a meaningful activity, such as a nature walk or volunteering, to deepen your sense of connection.

5. Practice forgiveness by letting go of one resentment or grudge this week.

Closing Thought

Spiritual growth and inner peace are not about escaping the challenges of life but about learning to navigate them with grace, resilience, and purpose. By turning inward and cultivating a sense of harmony within yourself, you can face the world with clarity and confidence. Remember, the path within is the most rewarding journey you'll ever take. Take the first step today.

"Allow your inner truth to shine; let vulnerability and respect merge, forging an intimacy that fuels both passion and growth."

INSPIRED BY MARK MANSON

Chapter

14:

Thriving Intimacy: A Guide to Sexual Health and Wellness

Sexual health is an essential component of overall well-being, yet it is often misunderstood or overlooked. Thriving intimacy goes beyond physical health it encompasses emotional, psychological, and relational aspects. This chapter focuses on understanding your body, building healthy attitudes toward intimacy, and nurturing meaningful connections through education, communication, and self-awareness.

Understanding Sexual Health

➡ **Defining Sexual Health:** A state of physical, emotional, mental, and social well-being concerning sexuality, not merely the absence of disease or dysfunction.

➡ **The Role of Sexual Wellness in Life:** Sexual health impacts confidence, relationships, and quality of life.

➡ **Destigmatizing Conversations About Sex:** Open, informed discussions help break taboos and promote healthier attitudes.

Step 1:

Educating Yourself on Sexual Health

1. **Know Your Anatomy**

> Understand the basic anatomy of your reproductive system and how it functions.

> Be aware of how age, lifestyle, and health conditions can impact sexual health.

2. **Stay Informed About Safe Practices**

> Learn about contraception options and their effectiveness in preventing unplanned pregnancies.

> Understand the importance of protecting against sexually transmitted infections (STIs) through safe practices like using condoms and regular testing.

3. **Seek Professional Guidance**

> Consult healthcare providers for questions about sexual health, performance, or concerns.

> Regular check-ups can help address issues early, from hormonal imbalances to fertility concerns.

Step 2:

Prioritizing Emotional and Mental Well-Being

1. **Addressing Shame or Guilt**

> Examine any cultural or personal beliefs that may create feelings of shame around intimacy.

> Replace judgment with self-compassion and a positive perspective on sexuality.

2. **Managing Stress and Anxiety**

> Stress is one of the leading causes of diminished sexual well-being. Practice stress-reduction techniques like mindfulness, exercise, or therapy.

> Understand the connection between mental health and physical intimacy.

3. **Exploring Your Relationship with Intimacy**

> Reflect on your desires, boundaries, and needs.

> Be honest with yourself about what intimacy means to you and how it fits into your overall life goals.

Building Healthy Relationships and Communication

1. **Open and Honest Communication**

> Discuss expectations, desires, and boundaries with your partner(s).

> Address issues like mismatched libido or unresolved conflict with empathy and understanding.

2. **Consent and Mutual Respect**

> Consent is the foundation of all healthy sexual relationships ensure all interactions are mutual and enthusiastic.

> Respect each other's boundaries and never pressure or coerce.

3. **Emotional Intimacy as a Foundation**

> Deepen emotional intimacy by fostering trust, vulnerability, and shared experiences.

> Emotional connection often enhances physical intimacy.

4. **Suppressing a Lustful Mind**

> Recognize Your Triggers: Identify situations, environments, or thoughts that fuel a lustful mindset and actively work to avoid or manage them.

> Shift Your Focus: Replace lustful thoughts with productive or meaningful activities such as exercise, hobbies, or pursuing personal goals.

Maintaining Physical Health for Thriving Intimacy

1. Exercise and Nutrition

> Regular exercise improves stamina, circulation, and energy levels, all of which benefit sexual health.

> Eat a balanced diet rich in nutrients that support hormonal balance and vitality, such as omega-3s, zinc, and magnesium.

2. Hormonal Health

> Be aware of hormonal changes that occur with age and lifestyle, and consult professionals for solutions like hormone therapy if necessary.

> Recognize symptoms of hormonal imbalances, such as fatigue, low libido, or mood swings.

3. Sleep and Rest

> Quality sleep is essential for sexual health, as it regulates hormone production and boosts energy.

> Avoid habits that disrupt sleep, such as excessive screen time or irregular sleep patterns.

Step 5:

Addressing Challenges and Seeking Solutions

1. Common Challenges

> Low libido, performance anxiety, or pain during intimacy are common but treatable issues.

> Don't ignore signs of dysfunction early intervention can often resolve problems.

2. Seek Professional Help

> Therapists or counselors specializing in sexual health can help address deeper issues.

> Medical professionals can provide solutions for physiological concerns, such as erectile dysfunction or hormonal imbalances.

3. Reframe Sexual Challenges as Opportunities for Growth

> Use challenges as an opportunity to grow closer to your partner through shared vulnerability and problem-solving.

Step 6:

Maintaining a Lifelong Healthy Attitude Toward Intimacy

1. Embrace Changing Dynamics

> Sexuality evolves due to age, health, and life circumstances.

> Adapt to changes with a positive outlook and a willingness to explore new forms of intimacy.

2. Continue Learning

> Stay informed about sexual health as new research, treatments, and resources emerge.

> Read books, attend workshops, or seek guidance to deepen your understanding.

3. Encourage Playfulness and Exploration

> Keep intimacy exciting by exploring new experiences and maintaining a sense of curiosity.

> Avoid falling into routines by introducing novelty in ways that feel comfortable and consensual.

Step 7:

Practicing Self-Love and Acceptance

1. Body Positivity

> Embrace your body as it is, focusing on its strengths and capabilities rather than perceived flaws.

> Challenge societal beauty standards that may negatively impact your self-image.

2. Masturbation as Self-Care

> Understand that masturbation is a normal and healthy aspect of sexuality, helping you learn about your body and preferences.

> Use it as a tool to relieve stress and build confidence in your intimacy, and not for lustful pleasures.

3. Prioritize Your Sexual Wellness

> Take the initiative to maintain your sexual health by staying active, educated, and attuned to your body's needs.

> Make self-care a priority, knowing that a healthy and confident you leads to better relationships.

Real-Life Example: Thriving Intimacy

Sexual health is a superpower-own it, protect it, and flaunt it. There was a time when I believed that prioritizing my sexual health was solely about having protected sex. However, as I delved deeper into understanding my well-being, I realized that true sexual health encompasses more than just routine check-ups and hygiene it's about promoting trust, respect, and open communication in every intimate relationship. I began scheduling regular health screenings, including comprehensive STD tests and blood work, four times a year. These appointments became more than just medical routines; they were affirmations of my commitment to myself and to those I chose to be intimate with. Maintaining meticulous personal hygiene and grooming further reinforced this commitment, ensuring that I presented my best self, both physically and emotionally.

Yet, the most transformative aspect of this journey was embracing open dialogue about sexual health with my partners. Initiating conversations about boundaries, expectations, and safe sex practices was initially daunting. However, I found that these discussions not only enhanced mutual understanding but also deepened the emotional connection. Research supports this, indicating that open communication about sexual health can significantly improve relationship satisfaction. By being proactive and transparent, I cultivated relationships rooted in trust and mutual respect. This approach not only safeguarded our physical health but also enriched our emotional bonds. I learned that true intimacy thrives when both partners feel safe, heard, and valued. In embracing this holistic view of sexual health, I discovered a deeper sense of self-awareness and confidence. It's a continuous journey, one that requires diligence, empathy, and open-heartedness. But the rewards authentic connections, peace of mind, and personal growth are immeasurable.

For anyone seeking to become a better man, remember: prioritizing your sexual health is not just about you. It's about honoring the well-being of those you care about and building relationships that are as healthy emotionally as they are physically. Sexual health is freedom-freedom to choose, to love, and to live authentically.

Action Plan:
Thriving Intimacy Checklist

1. Schedule an appointment with a healthcare professional to discuss your sexual health.

2. Dedicate time to reflect on your values, needs, and boundaries around intimacy.

3. Start a daily or weekly practice of mindfulness to reduce stress and increase self-awareness.

4. Plan an open conversation with your partner about intimacy goals, challenges, and desires.

5. Commit to regular physical activity and a balanced diet to enhance overall wellness.

Closing Thought

Thriving intimacy is about embracing your sexuality as a natural and enriching part of life. By prioritizing self-awareness, communication, and self-care, you can achieve a fulfilling, confident, and connected intimate life. Remember, sexual health and wellness are ongoing journeys that require attention, respect, and love for yourself and your partner. Always remember when choosing your partner. Quality over Quantity.

"*Every setback is a spark of potential; use challenges as stepping stones that propel you toward greatness.*"

INSPIRED BY MICHAEL JORDAN

Turning Challenges into Opportunities: Strengthening Your Conflict and Decision-Making Skills

Conflict and tough decisions are inevitable in life, but they don't have to be obstacles. Instead, they can become opportunities for growth, deeper understanding, and stronger relationships. This chapter will teach you how to approach conflicts constructively, improve your decision-making skills, and turn challenges into catalysts for success.

Understanding Conflict and Decision-Making

❯ **What Is Conflict?**

Conflict arises when two or more parties have differing needs, perspectives, or goals. It can be interpersonal, internal, or situational.

❯ **The Role of Decision-Making:**

Effective decisions provide solutions to conflicts and pave the way for progress. Poor decisions often exacerbate issues.

❯ **The Growth Opportunity:**

When handled well, conflict and decisions can lead to personal development, stronger relationships, and innovation.

Step 1:

Reframing Your Mindset About Conflict

1. **See Conflict as Neutral**
   - Conflict is neither inherently bad nor good it's how you handle it that determines its outcome.
   - Shift your mindset from "winning" to "resolving."

2. **Focus on the Opportunity**
   - Conflicts reveal underlying problems that need attention.
   - They provide a chance to clarify values, goals, and expectations.

3. Separate the Person from the Problem

> Avoid seeing the other party as an adversary. Address the issue without attacking the individual.

> This approach helps maintain respect and builds trust.

Step 2:

Key Skills for Conflict Resolution

1. Active Listening

> Listen to understand, not to reply.

> Paraphrase what the other person says to confirm understanding and show you're engaged.

2. Emotional Regulation

> Stay calm during heated moments. Take deep breaths or step away temporarily if needed.

> Avoid reacting impulsively, as this can escalate the situation.

3. Empathy and Perspective-Taking

> Put yourself in the other person's shoes to understand their perspective.

> Empathy helps build bridges and reduces defensiveness.

4. Communication with Clarity

> Use "I" statements (e.g., "I feel..." instead of "You always...") to express your needs without blaming.

> Be direct and specific about the issue and your desired outcome.

5. Problem-Solving Collaboration

> Work with the other person to brainstorm solutions.

> Focus on shared goals and compromises that benefit everyone involved.

Step 3:

Navigating Internal Conflict

1. Identifying the Source of Conflict

> Reflect on whether your conflict stems from misaligned goals, values, or emotions.

> Use journaling or mindfulness to gain clarity on your feelings and priorities.

2. Self-Compassion

> Avoid harsh self-criticism during internal struggles. Treat yourself with kindness and patience.

3. Aligning Actions with Values

> Evaluate whether your decisions align with your core values and long-term goals.

> Make adjustments to ensure consistency between your beliefs and actions.

Step 4:

Mastering Decision-Making

1. Define the Problem Clearly

> Articulate the issue you're trying to solve and why it's important.

> A clear definition sets the stage for effective decision-making.

2. Gather Information

> Avoid making decisions based on assumptions or incomplete information.

> Seek advice from trusted sources or conduct thorough research if necessary.

3. Evaluate Options Using Pros and Cons

> List the potential benefits and drawbacks of each option.

> Consider short-term and long-term impacts.

4. Trust Your Intuition

> While logic is important, don't ignore your gut feelings.

> Intuition often reflects deep-seated knowledge and experience.

5. Commit and Take Action

> Once a decision is made, act confidently. Avoid second-guessing yourself unless new information arises.

> Understand that no decision is perfect, and focus on moving forward.

6. The Importance of Patience

> Decision-making isn't always immediate and rushing can lead to poor outcomes.

> Allow yourself time to reflect on your options, especially for significant or high-stakes decisions.

> Patience creates space for clarity, helps manage emotions, and ensures that you are approaching decisions from a calm and rational state.

By practicing patience, you allow yourself to avoid impulsive choices and instead make thoughtful, deliberate decisions that align with your goals and values.

Step 5:

Say No to Negative Influences

➡ Recognize Harmful Patterns

> Identify individuals or environments that consistently drain your energy, undermine your confidence, or steer you away from your values.

> Acknowledge that not all relationships or situations are conducive to your growth and well-being.

➤ Set Clear Boundaries

> Establish and communicate personal limits to protect your mental and emotional health.

> Understand that it's okay to distance yourself from negativity, even if it means making difficult choices.

Never let anyone guilt trip you into making the wrong decision. Take 5-30 seconds to think about the consequences or reaction to your decision then choose your next action wisely.

➤ Cultivate a Positive Environment

> Surround yourself with people who inspire, support, and challenge you to be better.

> Engage in activities and communities that align with your aspirations and values.

Say "no" to organizations such as gangs and cults to protect your autonomy, uphold your values, and pursue a life of integrity and purpose. These groups often exploit vulnerabilities, offering a false sense of belonging or purpose, but ultimately seek to control and manipulate. By firmly rejecting their influence, you affirm your commitment to personal growth, authentic relationships, and a future defined by your own choices not by coercion or fear.

➤ Develop Assertiveness Skills

> Practice expressing your thoughts and decisions confidently and respectfully.

> Learn to say "no" when confronted with situations that contradict your values or compromise your well-being.

➤ Reflect and Adjust

> Regularly assess the influences in your life and their impact on your personal growth.

> Be willing to make necessary changes to maintain a supportive and empowering environment.

Turning Challenges into Opportunities

1. Learn from Every Conflict

> After resolving a conflict, reflect on what you learned about yourself, others, and the process.

> Use this knowledge to handle future conflicts more effectively.

2. Use Decision-Making as a Growth Tool

> Each decision you make builds your confidence and sharpens your problem-solving skills.

> Take risks when necessary, knowing that mistakes can lead to valuable lessons.

3. Strengthen Relationships Through Conflict

> Resolving conflict with respect and understanding often deepens trust and connection with others.

> Approach conflicts as opportunities to grow closer, not farther apart.

Avoiding Common Pitfalls

1. Emotional Reactivity

> Acting out of anger or frustration can damage relationships and lead to poor decisions.

> Take time to cool down before addressing conflict.

2. Avoiding Conflict

> Ignoring problems doesn't make them go away; it often makes them worse.

> Face conflicts head-on with a constructive attitude.

3. **Overthinking Decisions**

> Spending too much time analyzing every option can lead to paralysis by analysis.

> Set a reasonable deadline for making a decision and stick to it.

4. **Saying No**

> Recognizing Your Limits

> You can't do everything or please everyone saying yes to everything leads to burnout.

> Prioritize your time and energy for commitments that align with your values and goals.

> Overcoming the Fear of Disappointing Others

> Many people struggle to say no because they fear rejection or conflict.

> Understand that setting boundaries is not selfish it's necessary for self-respect and well-being.

> How to Say "No" with Confidence & Grace

> Be direct and polite: "I appreciate the offer, but I can't commit to this right now."

> Offer an alternative if appropriate: "I can't help with this, but I can suggest someone who might."

> Use firm but respectful body language and tone to reinforce your decision.

> The Long-Term Benefits of Saying No

> More time for meaningful activities and relationships.

> Increased self-respect and stronger personal boundaries.

> Less stress and resentment from overcommitting to things you don't truly want to do.

Saying no isn't about being difficult it's about protecting your time, energy, and mental well-being. The ability to decline distractions and unnecessary obligations allows you to focus on what truly matters.

Real-Life Example: Conflict Turned Opportunity

Challenges is life are inevitable but it's how we respond to them that makes all the difference As a former sales manager, I encountered many types of customers, including one particularly rude woman who arrived one day with a defensive tone and a bad attitude. My sales representative initially provided her with support, attempting to engage with her and address her concerns. However, as the interaction continued, her tone escalated she grew louder and increasingly aggressive toward my sales rep, and I could see that the rep was very close to matching the energy that the customer was putting out. Recognizing the rising tension, I stepped in to intervene, demonstrating how to deescalate the situation with empathy and a calm demeanor.

By remaining composed and using open body language alongside gentle tones, I created a safe space for her to lower her defenses. Gradually, her aggressive behavior softened, and she began engaging in a more meaningful dialogue. By the end of our interaction, not only had she transformed into a pleasant and cooperative customer, but she also expressed genuine gratitude for the patience and kindness I displayed, even offering to buy me lunch as a thank-you.

This experience reinforced the power of staying calm and showing empathy, turning a potentially negative encounter into an opportunity for connection and growth. It also provided my team with a live lesson in effective conflict resolution, demonstrating that a measured response can lead to positive outcomes even in challenging situations.

Empathy is a powerful tool in conflict resolution. By acknowledging and validating a person's feelings, we can de-escalate tense situations and build trust. As noted in the HEARD method, effective de-escalation involves hearing the person's concerns, empathizing with their feelings, apologizing for any inconvenience, resolving the issue, and diagnosing the problem to prevent future occurrences. By leading with empathy, we can transform challenging interactions into opportunities for growth and connection.

Action Plan: Building Your Conflict and Decision-Making Toolkit

1. Identify one recent conflict and analyze what worked and what didn't in resolving it.

2. Practice active listening in your next disagreement by summarizing the other person's points before responding.

3. Use the pros-and-cons method for a pending decision in your life.

4. Reflect on your core values and ensure your recent decisions align with them.

5. Commit to addressing one unresolved conflict this week with a calm, constructive approach.

Closing Thought

Conflict and decision-making are not just challenges they're opportunities to grow, strengthen relationships, and shape the life you want. By approaching them with clarity, empathy, and a solution-focused mindset, you can turn obstacles into stepping stones and emerge stronger and wiser. Every conflict resolved and decision made brings you one step closer to your goals. Embrace the process and keep moving forward.

"Modern chivalry shines through selfless acts; serve with a generous heart and let kindness light your way."

INSPIRED BY. ISAIAH REID

16:

Embracing Modern Chivalry: The Gentleman's Guide to Mastering the Art of Service

Modern chivalry is not about outdated customs or grandiose gestures it's about respect, kindness, and intentional actions that elevate others and reflect your character. True gentlemen understand that being of service is not an obligation but an honor. This chapter explores what it means to embody modern chivalry, teaching you how to lead with integrity, show respect, and make meaningful contributions to the lives of others.

Understanding Modern Chivalry

➲ What Is Modern Chivalry?

> A mindset rooted in respect, generosity, and selflessness.

> Focuses on uplifting others and building meaningful connections.

➲ Breaking Stereotypes:

> Modern chivalry isn't about rigid traditions it's about adapting timeless values to the world today.

> Anyone can practice chivalry, regardless of gender or background.

Step 1:

The Principles of Modern Chivalry

1. Respect for Everyone

> Treat people with dignity, regardless of their status or circumstances.

> Respect extends to your language, actions, and how you listen to others.

2. Genuine Kindness

> Perform acts of kindness without expecting anything in return.

> Small gestures, like holding a door or offering a kind word, can have a big impact.

3. Accountability in Your Actions

> Honor your commitments and take responsibility for your choices.

> A true gentleman owns up to mistakes and works to make amends.

4. Service as Leadership

> Service is not a weakness but a form of strength.

> Leading by serving others fosters trust and respect.

Step 2:

Practicing Chivalry in Everyday Life

1. Acts of Politeness and Consideration

> Hold doors open, but also respect others' autonomy don't assume they need help.

> Offer your seat on public transportation to those who might need it more.

2. Thoughtful Communication

> Address people politely, using titles like "sir" or "ma'am" where appropriate.

> Focus on being present in conversations put your phone away and give your undivided attention.

3. Helping Without Hesitation

> Look for opportunities to assist others, whether it's carrying groceries, volunteering, or offering advice.

> Be proactive in helping others succeed and celebrate their achievements.

Step 3:

The Gentleman's Guide to Relationships

1. Respect in Romantic Relationships

> Honor your partner's individuality and autonomy.

> Communicate openly and ensure that decisions are mutual.

> Simple gestures like pulling out a chair or planning thoughtful dates show effort and care. Don't let your woman touch any doors in your presence.

2. Elevating Friendships

> Be a dependable and supportive friend who listens and encourages.

> Offer help when needed, whether it's assisting with a project or being there during tough times.

3. Family and Community Engagement

> Show up for family events, lend a hand when needed, and be a source of positivity.

> Contribute to your community by volunteering, mentoring, or simply being neighborly.

Step 4:

Mastering the Art of Service

1. Develop a Servant-Leadership Mentality

> Great leaders serve others by creating environments where people can thrive.

> Prioritize the well-being and growth of those around you.

2. Practicing Gratitude

> Acknowledge the efforts and contributions of others regularly.

> Gratitude fosters humility and strengthens your relationships.

3. Pay It Forward

> When someone does something kind for you, look for ways to pass that kindness on to someone else.

> This creates a ripple effect of positivity.

Chivalry in the Modern World

1. **Adapting to Changing Social Norms**

    > Understand that some traditional gestures might not be welcomed by everyone always assess the situation.

    > When in doubt, ask or observe to ensure your actions are appreciated.

2. **Inclusivity in Chivalry**

    > Practice chivalry toward everyone, not just those you're romantically interested in.

    > Small gestures of kindness can uplift people from all walks of life.

3. **Technology and Modern Etiquette**

    > In the digital age, chivalry includes things like replying to messages promptly, avoiding rude behavior online, and using technology responsibly in social settings.

Examples of Modern Chivalry

1. **At Work:** A professional who regularly mentors junior employees, helping them grow and succeed without expecting credit.

2. **In Relationships:** A partner who plans thoughtful surprises for anniversaries or offers unwavering support during tough times.

3. **In the Community:** A volunteer who organizes local cleanups or contributes to charities, leading by example.

Overcoming Misconceptions About Chivalry

⮕ **Chivalry Isn't Outdated:** Some see chivalry as obsolete, but its principles are timeless.

⮕ **It's Not About Superiority:** Chivalry isn't about asserting dominance but about creating equality and respect.

⮕ **Service Is Strength:** Some view service as a weakness, but it requires courage, humility, and integrity.

Building a Legacy of Service

1. Inspiring Others

> When you embody chivalry, you encourage others to follow suit.

> A gentleman leads by example, showing the value of respect and kindness.

2. Leaving a Positive Impact

> Your actions, no matter how small, contribute to a better world.

> A gentleman's legacy is the lives he's touched and the kindness he's shown.

Knowing the Proper Etiquette of a Man

Social Interactions

1. **Stand to Greet:** Always rise when meeting someone new or greeting someone you respect.

2. **Firm Handshake with Eye Contact:** A confident handshake paired with eye contact conveys respect and sincerity.

3. **Use Names:** Remembering and using people's names in conversation shows attentiveness and respect.

4. **Introduce Others Properly:** When introducing people, mention the name of the person with higher status or age first.

5. **Mind Your Language:** Avoid offensive language and speak clearly and politely.

6. **Respect Personal Space:** Be mindful of others' personal space, especially in crowded settings.

Dining Etiquette

1. **Wait Before Eating:** Begin your meal only after everyone has been served and the host has started eating.

2. **Use Utensils Properly:** Start with the outermost utensils and work your way in with each course.

3. **Napkin Use:** Place your napkin on your lap upon sitting and use it to gently dab your mouth as needed.

4. **Chew with Mouth Closed:** Always chew quietly with your mouth closed and avoid talking with food in your mouth.

5. **Excuse Yourself Politely:** If you need to leave the table, do so quietly and excuse yourself to the group.

6. **Express Gratitude:** Thank your host and consider sending a follow-up note or message to express appreciation.

7. **Elbow Placement:** Your elbows should not rest on the table while dining.

Professional Etiquette

1. **Punctuality:** Arrive on time for meetings and appointments, showing respect for others' time.

2. **Dress Appropriately:** Adhere to the dress code of your workplace or event, ensuring a neat and professional appearance. No sagging your pants under any circumstances!

3. **Respect Confidentiality:** Keep company information and colleagues' personal matters private.

4. **Maintain Cleanliness:** Keep your workspace tidy and avoid eating strong-smelling foods at your desk.

5. **Positive Attitude:** Approach tasks with enthusiasm and be willing to assist colleagues when needed.

Gym Etiquette

1. **Wipe Down Equipment**: Always clean machines and benches after use to maintain hygiene.

2. **Return Weights:** Re-rack dumbbells and plates to their proper place after use.

3. **Limit Machine Time:** Be mindful of others waiting and avoid monopolizing equipment.

4. **Use Headphones:** Listen to music or videos through headphones to avoid disturbing others.

5. **Avoid Unsolicited Advice:** Offer help only if asked, respecting others' workout routines.

6. **Dress Appropriately:** Wear clean, suitable workout attire and appropriate footwear.

Event Etiquette

1. RSVP Promptly: Respond to invitations in a timely manner, using the method specified.

2. Be a Gracious Guest: Show appreciation for hospitality and avoid criticizing the host's efforts.

3. Avoid Overstaying: Be mindful of the time and leave at an appropriate hour to respect your host's schedule.

4. Engage in Conversation: Participate in discussions, showing interest in others' viewpoints.

5. Offer Assistance: If appropriate, help the host with tasks like setting the table or cleaning up.

6. Follow Up: Send a thank-you note or message after the event to express your gratitude.

Digital Etiquette

1. **Mind Your Tone**
- > **Avoid All Caps:** Typing in all capital letters can be perceived as shouting.
- > **Be Clear and Concise:** Ensure your messages are straightforward to prevent misunderstandings.

2. **Respect Privacy**
- > **Think Before Sharing:** Avoid forwarding messages or sharing information without consent.
- > **Be Cautious with Personal Details:** Protect your own and others' personal information online.

3. **Professional Communication**
- > **Use Proper Grammar and Spelling:** This reflects professionalism and respect.

> **Respond Promptly:** Timely responses show consideration for others' time.

> **Email Courtesy:** Respond to emails promptly and maintain a professional tone.

4. Appropriate Use of Platforms

> **Know Your Audience:** Tailor your communication style to suit different platforms and audiences.

> **Avoid Spamming:** Refrain from sending unsolicited messages or excessive postings.

Travel Etiquette

1. At the Airport

> **Be Prepared:** Have your documents ready and follow security procedures efficiently.

> **Respect Personal Space:** Maintain appropriate distance in lines and waiting areas.

2. On the Plane

> **Board and Disembark Considerately:** Allow others to exit before boarding and retrieve your items swiftly to avoid delays.

> **Mind Your Seat:** Recline seats gently and be aware of the space you're occupying.

3. Public Transportation

> **Offer Seats:** Give up your seat to those in need, such as the elderly or pregnant individuals.

> **Keep Noise Levels Down:** Use headphones and keep conversations at a low volume.

4. General Conduct

> **Be Punctual:** Arrive on time for departures to avoid inconveniencing others.

> **Dress Appropriately:** Wear suitable attire that respects local customs and norms.

Timeless Wisdom

1. **Practice Self-Control:** Manage your impulses and behave with dignity in all situations.

2. **Show Respect to All:** Treat everyone with courtesy, regardless of their status or relationship to you.

3. **Lead by Example:** Demonstrate the behavior you expect from others through your own actions.

4. **Maintain Integrity:** Be honest and uphold strong moral principles in all dealings.

5. **Cultivate Empathy:** Understand and share the feelings of others to build strong relationships.

6. **Continuous Improvement:** Seek personal growth and learning opportunities to better yourself.

Action Plan:
Becoming a Modern Gentleman

1. Start each day by asking yourself, "How can I be of service to someone today?"

2. Perform one selfless act daily no matter how small.

3. Practice active listening in all your interactions this week.

4. Reflect on how you can be more supportive and dependable in your relationships.

5. Look for a way to give back to your community, such as volunteering or donating.

Real-Life Example:
A True Gentleman

Every morning, as I step into the world, I carry with me a commitment to uphold the values of a gentleman. It's in the simple gestures: holding the door open for someone, offering a seat to the elderly, or lending a listening ear to a friend in need. These acts, though small, are profound expressions of empathy and respect. I recall a moment when I assisted an elderly neighbor with her groceries. Her eyes sparkled with gratitude, and she shared stories of her youth, reminding me of the rich tapestry of experiences that each person carries. Such interactions reinforce my belief that chivalry is not about grandiose acts but about recognizing and honoring the humanity in others.

Chivalry, in its modern form, transcends outdated notions of gender roles. It's about fostering an environment where everyone feels valued and respected. As highlighted in discussions on modern chivalry, it's about treating everyone with dignity, acting with integrity, and constantly improving oneself. In my interactions, I strive to embody this ethos. Whether it's mentoring young men on the importance of empathy or ensuring that the elderly in my community feel seen and heard, these actions are rooted in a deep-seated respect for others.

One of the most fulfilling aspects of embracing modern chivalry is the opportunity to mentor others. By sharing experiences and lessons learned, I aim to guide others in understanding that being a gentleman is synonymous with strength, respect, and self-assurance. Mentorship is not about dictating behavior but about modeling values. It's about demonstrating that true confidence comes from humility, that leadership is rooted in service, and that integrity is the cornerstone of lasting relationships.

Every act of kindness sets off a ripple effect, influencing not just the immediate recipient but also those who witness it. By consistently practicing chivalry, we contribute to a culture of compassion and mutual respect. Incorporating these values into daily life doesn't require monumental changes. It's about being present, attentive, and willing to act in service of others. As we each take on the mantle of modern chivalry, we collectively move towards a more empathetic and respectful society.

Embracing modern chivalry is a conscious choice to live with purpose and integrity. It's about recognizing that our actions, no matter how small, have the power to uplift others and transform communities. By committing to the principles of respect, kindness, and service, we not only honor the legacy of the gentleman but also pave the way for a more compassionate future. Let us, therefore, wear the badge of a gentleman with pride, knowing that in doing so, we contribute to a world where dignity and empathy reign supreme.

Closing Thought

Modern chivalry is a commitment to serve, respect, and uplift others. It's about embodying values that inspire trust, love, and admiration. By mastering the art of service, you don't just enhance your character you leave a legacy of kindness and integrity that will ripple through the lives of others. Start today, and watch how small acts of service can transform your world.

"*Every choice you make is a brushstroke on your legacy paint boldly with passion, purpose, and a desire to inspire.*"

INSPIRED BY LEONARDO DA VINCI

Chapter 17:

Defining Your Legacy: Creating a Lasting Impact on the World

The journey to becoming a better man is not just about self-improvement; it's about how you shape the world around you. Your legacy is the sum of the values you live by, the actions you take, and the lives you touch. This chapter is about looking forward embracing the responsibility and opportunity to leave a positive mark on the world.

As you read this final chapter, take a moment to appreciate how far you've come. This book has guided you through reinvention, discipline, emotional growth, and service. Now, it's time to put it all together and focus on your ultimate purpose: creating a legacy of meaning, integrity, and impact.

What Is a Legacy?

❯ **More Than Material Wealth:** Your legacy isn't just about what you achieve or accumulate but the values and lessons you pass down.

❯ **How You Influence Others:** A legacy lives in the relationships you nurture, the communities you serve, and the people you inspire.

❯ **A Story You Write Daily:** Your legacy is a reflection of your actions, decisions, and how you make others feel.

Step 1:

Living with Purpose

1. **Clarify Your Core Values**

   > Identify the principles that define who you are and guide your life.

   > Examples include integrity, compassion, resilience, and service.

   > Write these values down and evaluate whether your daily actions align with them.

2. **Establish Your Mission**

   > What impact do you want to have on your family, community, and the world?

   > Your mission should be rooted in your passions and your desire to create change.

3. **Set Long-Term Goals**
> Define what success means to you.
> Whether it's raising a strong family, building a business that helps others, or mentoring the next generation, let your goals reflect your legacy.

Step 2:

Making a Positive Impact

1. **Start with Small Acts of Kindness**
> Simple gestures, like offering a helping hand or encouraging words, create ripples of positivity.
> Consistent kindness builds a reputation for thoughtfulness and care.

2. **Invest in Relationships**
> Your legacy is deeply tied to how you treat others.
> Prioritize listening, showing empathy, and being present for the people who matter most.

3. **Contribute to Your Community**
> Volunteer your time, share your skills, or support causes that align with your values.
> Strengthening your community strengthens your legacy.

Step 3:

Inspiring the Next Generation

1. **Be the Example**
> Your actions set the tone for those who look up to you.
> Show courage, humility, and integrity in how you live.

2. **Share Your Knowledge**
>   Pass down lessons you've learned through your experiences.
>   Mentor younger individuals to guide them through challenges.

3. **Prioritize Family Legacy**
>   Spend time teaching your children or loved ones the values you hold dear.
>   Create traditions and memories that will live on for generations.

Step 4:

Overcoming Challenges to Leave a Positive Legacy

1. **Learn from Mistakes**
>   No one's journey is perfect. Use failures as opportunities to grow and refine your impact.
>   Apologize and make amends when necessary.

2. **Focus on What Matters Most**
>   Avoid distractions that pull you away from your purpose.
>   Stay grounded in your mission and values, even when life gets busy.

3. **Stay Resilient**
>   Challenges will arise, but your ability to push through them will inspire others.
>   Every setback is an opportunity to demonstrate strength and character.

Action Plan:
Building Your Legacy

1. **Define Your Legacy Statement:** Write a brief description of the impact you want to leave behind.

2. **Evaluate Your Daily Actions:** Reflect on whether your actions align with your desired legacy.

3. **Contribute to a Cause:** Choose one way to give back, whether it's volunteering, mentoring, or supporting a cause.

4. **Strengthen a Relationship:** Reach out to someone important to you and show gratitude or support.

5. **Write Your Story:** Begin documenting your values, experiences, and lessons to share with others.

Step 5:

Have Fun with Life

Life isn't just about responsibilities, discipline, and legacy it's also about enjoyment, laughter, and making memories. Too often, men get caught up in the pressures of work, success, and self-improvement, forgetting the importance of simply having fun. Embracing joy and adventure leads to a more fulfilling and well-rounded life.

1. **The Importance of Having Fun**
> Boosts Mental & Emotional Health
> Engaging in fun activities reduces stress, anxiety, and burnout.
> Laughter releases endorphins, which improve mood and overall well-being.
> Strengthens Relationships
> Sharing enjoyable experiences deepens connections with family, friends, and loved ones.

- Having fun with others fosters stronger bonds and creates lasting memories.
- Increases Creativity & Productivity
- Taking time to relax and play boosts problem-solving skills and creative thinking.
- Fun activities provide a mental reset, helping you return to work with fresh energy.
- Enhances Overall Life Satisfaction
- A life filled with joy, adventure, and new experiences leads to greater fulfillment.
- Fun isn't a distraction from success it's an essential part of a well-lived life.

2. How to Make Life More Fun

- Prioritize Hobbies & Passions
- Set aside time for activities that bring you genuine happiness, whether it's sports, music, gaming, or outdoor adventures.
- Try new experiences step out of your routine and explore different interests.
- Surround Yourself with Playful, Positive People
- Spend time with those who bring laughter and excitement into your life.
- Engage in social activities that encourage fun and spontaneity.
- Embrace Adventure & Spontaneity
- Travel to new places, even if it's just a weekend getaway.
- Say yes to experiences that push you out of your comfort zone.
- Don't Take Life Too Seriously
- Learn to laugh at yourself and find humor in everyday situations.
- Release the pressure to always be perfect mistakes and surprises are part of the journey.

3. **The Long-Term Benefits of Enjoying Life**

> **Better Mental & Physical Health:** Reduced stress leads to lower blood pressure, improved heart health, and a longer lifespan.

> **Stronger Social Connections:** Shared fun moments create meaningful and lasting friendships.

> **Increased Resilience:** A joyful mindset helps you navigate challenges with a more positive outlook.

> **A Balanced Life:** Success isn't just about work it's about living with passion, adventure, and excitement.

LIFE IS MEANT TO BE
enjoyed.

Taking time for fun doesn't mean you're being irresponsible it means you're embracing all aspects of life.
Work hard, grow, and strive for greatness, but never forget to smile, laugh, and create unforgettable memories along the way.

A Message of
GRATITUDE

Thank you for embarking on this journey of self-discovery and growth. Your commitment to becoming a better man speaks volumes about your character. This book was written with the hope of inspiring change, and the fact that you've reached this final chapter is a testament to your determination and courage.

As you move forward, remember that the journey never truly ends. Each day is an opportunity to grow, to serve, and to inspire. The world needs more men like you men who strive to leave a legacy of love, integrity, and purpose.

A Personal Message
FROM ISAIAH

Congratulations on completing this book and taking the steps to become a better man. You've faced challenges, reflected on your values, and committed to personal growth and that is no small task.

As you define your legacy, remember that it's not about being perfect. It's about showing up every day with intention, learning from your mistakes, and making a positive impact on the lives of others.

I'm proud of the progress you've made, and I believe in the incredible future you're building. Continue to embrace growth, live with purpose, and lead with love. The world is better because of men like you.

Thank you for allowing me to be part of your journey. Now, go out and leave your mark.

Sincerely,
Isaiah

www.ingramcontent.com/pod-product-compliance
Lightning Source LLC
Chambersburg PA
CBHW051309120626
46547CB00015B/2149